HERE TODAY AND *PERHAPS* TOMORROW

and Die Laughing in a Retirement Community

Peter William Kent

Portraits of Elderly Care

outskirtspress
DENVER, COLORADO

"Age is like a mountain top high,
rarer the air and blue,
A long hard climb,
a bit of fatigue,
But Oh, what a wonderful view!"
—Anonymous

To Dear Clare with My Love

This book is dedicated to my fiancée, Clare Maria Hunter. We both live in a California retirement community. I am of retirement age. Clare does not look a day over thirty-four, and I do not look a day over retirement age.

Clare persuaded me to write an enlightening book about retirement communities. She saw this book in me and offered strong encouragement to start writing. We often shared feelings about retirement since we live in the same building, and have experienced much of the same drama. Genteel debate is part of both our natures. One sunny day she told me to stop watching TV and start writing a book. I did, and thank her very much. Clare has been a wise and patient editor, an inspiration, and a powerful motivator. I have appreciated her literary ideas.

Table of Contents

"Regular naps sustain old age, unless you take one while driving."
—Author unknown

ACKNOWLEDGMENTS

I am indebted to Clare, my sweetheart and accomplice, as well as to Betsy, my daughter.

Clare has supported me with her patience, enthusiasm and loving guidance. She gave me valuable editing help, as we reflected on elderly living in a retirement community setting. She was invaluable. Betsy became an accomplished proofreader. Her occasional visits remind me that families can be a secure deliverance during long spells of retirement community living.

My appreciation to Outskirts Press, my publisher. Lisa Jones and Sheri Breeding rendered professional assistance. They provided wise counsel, sound suggestions, and useful publication support. Lisa, your patience is appreciated.

Egle Bartolini Pensa is an accomplished cartoonist. He expertly responded to my desire for occasional diversion. It was not hard to describe my cartoon needs to this pleasant Italian who lives in northern Italy. I appreciate his cartoons. They poke fun and lighten the narrative.

My gratitude to Margaret Griffin, President of CALCRA, Quelda Wilson, a resident council president, and Bill Sciortino in Chicago. They provided helpful ideas that kept me focused. Many thank.

A key to successful retirement community life requires the cultivation of positive relationships with the residents and community staff. A key to successful writing is to get help from relatives, friends, and a publisher.

Any incident or person in this book that appears familiar to a reader is a complete coincidence. A perceived likeness in the book's cartoons to persons living or dead is purely accidental and unintended. I present a broad landscape of the American continuing care retirement community setting. Retirement living is an ever evolving episode of life's experiences.

Peter William Kent

"There goes Irving showing off again . . . ."

"Sometimes it takes years to really grasp what happened in your life."
—Wilma Rudolph

CHAPTER ONE

ELDERLY VIEWPOINTS

How do you prefer to be cared for during the remaining retirement years of your life?

This book is about the elderly, and those who become infirm. It provides readers with greater insight into a particular approach to elderly living. In addition, it comments on several features of this mode of retirement life. It characterizes the elderly, including their good cheer, their biases, and their wisdom. Retirees have many lifestyle choices, and act on them. Few of these choices are ever included in juveniles' aspirations.

Retirement facilities come in many shapes and sizes, as do all retirees. On occasion retirees have been vaguely compared to old wines. Old wines, like the elderly, spend a long time getting old. Wines, like retirees, are enjoyed by some and disapproved of by others. Wine flavors can be pleasing or displeasing, especially after reaching a ripe old age. Older wine occasionally turns to vinegar. Retirees occasionally become vinegary. Compassionate caring for the elderly varies by labeling and the degree of maturity. The older the wine the better it may become. At some point, wines do slide downhill.

Retirement facilities can get wobbly, particularly when a preferred Chardonnay runs out in the bar. Residents will enjoy the best of all worlds if their community has a dining-room liquor license. Managing such wobbly situations is a delicate art. Wines occasionally produce wobbly retirees. In short, wines and retirement community residents seem to be closely linked, especially during happy hours.

This book may mean more to readers who end up with added knowledge of retirement community people and their environments. The contents may be of value to someone who reads the book, and then becomes more convinced he did the right thing by moving into a retirement facility. It can reinforce a son's confidence after he moved his mother into such a community. It might better educate a widow and help her make a more informed decision about embracing the retirement community concept. Alternatively, it may validate a couple's decision to continue living in the home they have owned for thirty years, rather than relocate to a retirement community. Another reader will forward his copy of this book to a neighbor suggesting he read it before signing a move-in contract. Other readers will only chuckle.

There are a number of published books about retirement community facilities. Many of them conscientiously attempt to tackle diverse retirement facility features and benefits such as locality, costs, service, food, apartment size, caregiving, and proximity to a lively mortuary. Such retirement "guidebooks" can provide information about a host of communities from coast to coast. Facilities are assessed and described to readers for their review, approval, or disapproval. They provide information about geographic locations, the size of communities, services offered, and so on. Books on overseas retirement facilities are available. Retirement guidebooks provide their readers with a great deal of pragmatic information about retirement communities. This is not such a book. It is certainly not a retiree guidebook. It is not even a tongue-in-cheek guidebook.

Retirees have occasionally benefited from different career paths during their working lives. They busied themselves in various occupations. Jobs changed after they had been laid off, promoted, or moved on to a better opportunity. In one way or another we have all been achievers. We carved out careers in business, the military, medicine, education, etc. Resumes detailed many accomplishments.

I experienced several careers during my business life and retired three times. With a single exception, all this work experience was of minor relevance in helping me write this book. That exception was my professional background in diagnosing organization behavior and developing people change strategies. At one time I became a management consultant, which included providing these services to a large Hospice organization. All this was pertinent work experience supporting my enthusiasm for writing about seniors and their community lives.

Being quite elderly is a second qualification for writing a book about residing in a particular type of retirement community. As I wrote, I was able to reflect on almost twelve years of exposure to the continuing care retirement community setting. My narratives ponder on happenings at more than one retirement community for the elderly. I reflect on situations that have occurred over an extended period of time.

Both of these personal attributes are called on to write this book.

The book focuses on three areas of interest.

- Retirees living in continuing care retirement communities.
- Managers and other employees who work in such communities.
- Various external environmental entities that impact community residents.

Some retirees relish style in their retirement, with the accompanying luxury. This may have significance to a few individuals who want to be perceived as socially successful and worldly during their end-of-life experiences. They may appreciate a more refined lifestyle with its sophisticated facilities and extensive menus.

The caliber of institutional caregiving varies considerably. Many facilities offer basic services. Some possess less well-trained staffs. Others are on the verge of losing their certification. There are places for millionaires and places for residents who are broke and on Medicaid. The former certainly do provide a wider range of attractive facilities. The outcome for such contrasting and diverse groups of residents is perfectly identical. What a shame.

Retirees often choose to live out their lives in their own homes. This can be risky as frailty progresses, and might eventually require considerable personal resources for long term skilled, and other supportive care at home. Some retirees wait too long to move into a retirement community, and are then denied entry. Remember, some elderly citizens simply linger, and even endure.

A retiree may be perfectly happy living in an upstairs bedroom, alongside his family. In time, caregiver patience and happiness can burn out. As a consequence, family members might resort to a round-robin caregiving strategy. They shuffle poor mother from son to daughter and then on to another son. This may not help the conscience.

Elderly community living has matured within a mélange of caregiving options. The community living style has successfully filled gaps in providing elderly healthcare. In spite of its perceived complexities, the community world is not as topsy-turvy as one can imagine.

The reader needs to know that from time to time the author had to place a hold on writing this book. He was obligated to make several visits to a local emergency room and hospital. He became increasingly sensitive to the benefits of skilled nursing facilities. Healthcare would eventually become an increasing part of his regimen. Somehow old age can do that. Ailments keep the elderly off their feet and periodically on their toes. The author confidently faced these challenges. Each time he returned to finish this book titled, *Here Today and Perhaps Tomorrow*.

This volume is about continuing care retirement communities for old folks predisposed to a more elegant retirement lifestyle. It is not a definitive review of retirement community standards or concepts as a whole. If the reader wants more about that he should go to the Internet, visit a library, or read another retirement book. But only after he has read *Here Today and Perhaps Tomorrow* from cover to cover.

We only die once, which is terribly unfair. In fact, this situation alarms too many human beings. In spite of this, the reader will not be presented with a sense of foreboding or doom. The book is sanguine. It avoids conscious prejudice and includes a more entertaining outlook about retirement living. It only includes one feeble joke about the elderly.

Poking fun at an old lady trying to cope with Alzheimer's disease can be insensitive, to say the least. Nonetheless, it does have a humorous and tongue-in-cheek quality. It periodically chides the medical profession and the skilled nursing facilities of continuing care retirement communities in particular. Once in a while it has a more serious tone. It scrutinizes some aspects of legislative actions and public affairs that align with the retirement community business. It harps on some aspect of social injustice, arbitrary public practices and offers thoughts about skilled caregiving.

Genuine good humor is a common retirement community denominator. This is where the book periodically contributes the most. Tolerance and humor permeate even the dreariest of retirement environments. Perhaps we need to chuckle more about all the predicaments we experience within the humdrum of retirement living. The reader is presented with a series of short stories and observations about the elderly. They describe the nuisances of this community life and its environment. Included are descriptions of people situations as they age in style. The book does not establish any clear benchmarks or mandatory standards pertaining to retirement life. I leave that up to others.

A review of the literature shows that the social side of retirement community life is not always well described to the public. Many books simply describe the bricks and mortar aspects of facilities, and the extent of care. A goal of this book is to provide the reader with more insight into the practicality, nuances, and behaviors of community living. It is not a comprehensive study of retirement community investments, business planning, occupancy rates, or financial strategies. Neither is it intended to be a behavioral research study on the feelings, comparative resident attitudes, morale, or resident satisfaction. It has an anecdotal thread. Reader knowledge is a good thing. Retirement community knowledge, when clearly imparted to the elderly, is a very good thing.

Little humor presents itself when a writer single-mindedly tracks operational data, room sizes, and contract terms. This book recognizes that residents have attitudes, emotions, and feelings. Narratives are associated with a panorama of happenings, inside and outside several facilities. This landscape provides fuel for the book's vignettes, anecdotes, and narratives. The author has drawn on personal observations and research. Some vagaries of retirement living are documented.

The book contains a rare rebuke. It does not want to point fingers. Within its collection of anecdotes and revelations, the book refers to, and even argues about, the singularity of the skilled nursing center. In this context, the spotlight of an occasional admonition is directed towards this important component of continuing care retirement communities. Long term skilled nursing is sometimes the bane of the functionality of these communities. Patient attitudes and infirmity can severely tax the responsibility to maintain a complete health-care program.

I avoid reprimanding CCRC managements, and pass on scolding community residents. It must be realized that professional caregivers do burn out while the latter do experience enough difficulties coping with the wandering course of their ageing. Things can be demanding enough in this living environment.

The book might clearly describe the remaining years of a reader's life. It paints a noteworthy picture of continuing care retirement community living. It will look at the serious task of facility management. It makes no recommendations.

"It is always easy to be logical. It is almost impossible to be logical to the bitter end."
— Albert Camus

CHAPTER TWO

THE RELATIONSHIP BETWEEN PEOPLE AND THINGS IN RETIREMENT COMMUNITY LIVING

This section presents an environmental concept of the retirement community setting. It looks at two very real and contrasting dimensions that pervade residents' lives and community living. This living dichotomy will now be described by examining two distinct aspects of the retirement community milieu. Each may be characterized in terms of:

- The **PEOPLE** side of retirement communities,

AND

- The **THINGS** side of retirement organizations and their environments.

For clarification, these two aspects or notions are portrayed in the four following descriptive narratives.

I. The *People* side of retiree environments refers to individuals, their behaviors and their interactions within a retirement community environment. *People* can exhibit passionate feelings, emotions, and levels of energy. They have attitudes within an extended world of caring. This *people* side of retirement life is characterized in the following two situational examples

I. a. An extract from a Presentation delivered by a Psychologist during a Retiree Caregiving Seminar.

"In summary, many retirees worry about their loneliness. The economics of retirement gives pause to many, particularly over the loss of spouses, or their capital. Many feel anxious about the beginnings of memory loss. Poor health is a frequent worry. Recuperation from illness becomes an increasing challenge with ageing. Old age demands courage. Optimism prevails. It is very normal for individuals to search for answers to their difficulties. Many residents turn towards us and the Almighty."

1. b. A Retirement Community announcement on residents' activities.

The following community bulletin informs residents about current and planned social happenings in their facility.

"THE RESIDENTS' WEEKLY COMMUNITY REMINDER

We are delighted to announce the winners of last week's leading social and sports activities.

GOLF: Mr. Adrian Fellows
DUPLICATE BRIDGE: Mr. and Ms. Walter Keller
BINGO: Ms. Bernice Springstein
THE WEEKLY QUIZ: Ms. Ellen Albertini
BOWLING: Mr. Joseph Fallini
PING PONG: Ms. Estelle Rodriguez
DRAMARIC READINGS: Mr. Steve Forkman

ADDITIONAL ANNOUNCEMENTS

Dr. John Lewis will speak on Stenosis and the Spine on March 6th. at 3 pm. in the living room.

Do not forget the presentation by Dr. Henry Felmig on "The Making of the Universe."
Tuesday, March 15th. at 9:00 am in the living room.

Ms. Doris Bennett will present her paintings in the living room all day next Monday, March 29th.

The cooking class has been rescheduled to Tuesday, March, 30th, starting at 10:00 am in the kitchen.

Congratulations to the Activities Committee for organizing the needlepoint classes!

Thank you.

The Recreation Staff."

II. The highly contrasting nature of the next two quotations signifies the reality that retirement communities do operate in broader social contexts. These encompass such areas as operational procedures and practices, the organization structure, profits and operating systems. This is characterized as the *Things* side of organizations, and their influences, which both focus on more inanimate aspects of the retirement environment. It includes such areas as the number of residents in a community, the size of apartments, staffing levels, medical care, relevant legislation, government regulations, advocacy, resident policies and food.

Listed below are two examples that demonstrate this category. They were excerpted from retirement trade magazines. Both illustrate the *Things* side of the retirement community environment. They co-exist with the *People* side.

II. a. A Retirement Industry Planning Report making recommendations to executives intent on starting a retirement community business.

"Perhaps you are concerned about taking care of the elderly, and you wish to start a business. Your goals should focus on providing seniors with a comfortable, exciting, and active lifestyle. Your functional education should begin by designing and planning a retirement community operation. Developing such a facility involves such areas as design and construction, plus needing knowledge in project management. It would be beneficial for you to visit some retirement facilities. Your education and training must include college courses in community design, planning, and real estate development. You should attend seminars highlighting issues concerning the development of senior communities."

II. b. A Business Planning Report containing a message to entities wishing to develop an exit strategy from their retirement community business.

"Good business plans include a section that lays out the benchmarks you will use in deciding to exit your business. Your strategy must be based on a dollar cost figure, revenue data, the market's reception to your move, and a consensus among your top officers. Sensitivity to residents' needs is vital."

Both dimensions, as described here, always influence each other in the retirement community setting. *People* elements are involved in the *Things* aspects of occurrences in a community environment. In the same way, *Things* are simultaneously involved in the *People* side. They are not isolated. Both are recognized by their core focus. They are concomitantly portrayed throughout this book. As readers absorb the contents of **Here Today and Perhaps Tomorrow**, they will better understand the integration of both dimensions of retirement life.

In a more lighthearted fashion, this dual faceted approach to describe the retirement community environment may be characterized by two down-to-earth definitions.

1. Serious efforts to describe some salient aspects of the public and private aspects of the retirement community business by weaving them around pictures of *People* living in a retirement community surrounding.

OR

2. Tongue-in-cheek efforts to describe some salient aspects of the entertaining pictures of residents living in

retirement communities by weaving them around serious narratives that describe the *Things* elements of the private and public facets in the retirement business.

Having identified the scope of the book's contents, the writer consulted with several of his retirement community friends. He requested their opinions about any optional approaches he might employ to express his ideas and narratives to the reader. After all they clearly understood retirement living as well as he did. They had also endorsed this way of life.

One person counseled that the book must have two entirely separate sections. The first would include harebrained stories about retirement communities. The second should include serious narratives about community managements and related retirement organizations. There would be no linkage between the two.

The author earnestly argued that the community retirement experience and environment are best described when different, yet connected, dimensions are realistically presented. They can be depicted alongside each other since this is how real life happens. In other words, sensitivity to the relationship of people and things.

In contrast, another friend suggested the book must contain a potpourri of retirement narratives. They should be randomly written in a single volume containing a continuous sequence of narratives. I was concerned that such a complete and indiscriminate mélange would give the impression that retirement community living is perplexing.

A third person suggested the author should produce two books. One must be funny. The other would examine the serious business aspects of retirement living. This *people* and *things* approach made some sense. Yet both are particularly closely connected in the retirement culture. But what if I succumbed to Alzheimer's disease prior to finishing the detailed scientific analysis to complete the *Things* book? I simply needed to get moving telling a story.

So I decided to write a single and carefully organized book that focused on my perceptions of *people* and *things*, and contained depictions of retirement. This included thoughts and observations about elderly living in retirement community surroundings. It would include the operational environment. It must incline to be both witty and serious, and recognize the salient aspects of broad and vital retirement settings. The book would then provide greater insight into the diverse dimensions of continuing care retirement community living. It would avoid leaving readers with the impression that retirement communities are funny farms.

This is why I wrote a uniquely researched book, and selected its distinctive style. I wanted to cause readers to be increasingly sensitive to elderly feelings and their social environment. I wanted to do this in a more refreshing and revealing way. Perhaps I sometimes wanted to gently remind managers of retirement facilities that things can always be improved!

After reading this book, old and new residents, geriatrics researchers, the prospective resident, as well as non-resident, will be more cognizant of a distinct retiree environment. They will be more aware of the background and dynamics of an exceptionally fine version of retirement living.

"Age is an issue of mind over matter.
If you don't mind, it doesn't matter."
—Mark Twain

CHAPTER THREE

RETIREMENT LIVING IS A LIFESTYLE

THE WORLD OF THE CCRC

Continuing Care Retirement Communities offer a haven for relatively healthy and slightly debilitated seniors who exceed a designated age. Senior citizens seek to reduce their anxiety over where they will live during particularly old age. Residents of continuing care facilities typically worry less about how to cope with future illnesses and frailties of extreme old age. Several levels of caregiving are available to residents of these communities. More on that later.

The book is about CCRCs, which is an easier way to refer to Continuing Care Retirement Communities. The acronym is a concise way of identifying a particular type of retirement property, and style of elderly living.

I live in a CCRC. The company that owns my CCRC is a com-petent, and a relatively small entity in a large nation-wide retirement community property market. During the past forty years, such communities have become an essential part of the American retirement scene. One such community, located in California, has been in this kind of retirement business for over a hundred years.

The CCRC mode has two different methods of operation. There are for-profit and not-for-profit properties. The latter includes a number of socially conscious organizations, such as a religious denomination. It may be said that non-profit operations strive more eagerly to meet the need for elderly care and have a strong social conscience. This assertion cannot ignore the positive motives, good caring, and attitudes of for-profit entities.

There are many strong proponents of faith-embedded CCRC living. Other entities deserve equally serious consideration. Those in favor profess that faith centered non-profit CCRCs offer more sympathetic residential care and are more responsive to residents' needs. Those in favor of for-profits may suggest their residences are more financially efficient and productive in the business of providing elderly care. The arguments go on.

Trust is at the root of fulfilling obligations for senior care whether for-profit or not-for-profit. It also depends on the extent of caring and the sound business practices employed by either type of community. In the final analysis, not-for-profit businesses must meet or exceed their financial targets. Simply meeting most operating priorities is insufficient. We might say that both types of operations are actually for-profit. Then there are the issues around tax exemptions for non-profits and the tax-paying burdens of for-profits. These topics are well left for another book.

A review of the care components of continuing care retirement communities follows. These brief descriptions are provided so less informed readers can become better informed on the CCRC's multi-caring approach.

A CLARIFICATION OF THE LEVELS OF CCRC CARE
FOR THE LESS INFORMED

Elderly care and retirement communities are components of healthcare. Some individuals consider our current national healthcare policies and services to be acceptable operational accomplishments. To others they are another bugled element of the public health system. Public policy debates on healthcare issues are lively and endless. Discussions occasionally arouse passionate feelings. Opinions on alternative styles of retirement living are plentiful.

Retirement communities are a segment of the business of caring for an elderly clientele. They are rarely of interest to the younger population. An occasional high school student might be asked to prepare a term paper on this topic. This student might eventually become even more sensitive about a relative in a retirement community. These retirement facilities are of far greater importance to the elderly. They can be of inconsistent interest to politicians.

CCRCs take care of the elderly as their resources will allow. Some retirees are convinced these facilities will entirely meet their old age needs. Others will prefer to remain in their homes for their remaining years. A recent survey by the Met. Life Mature Market Institute indicated that 83 percent of individuals reaching retirement age do not plan to leave their current residence. So the elderly will investigate retirement community living and reject moving in, or they will conduct their research and relocate. The former are the principal segment of the elderly population.

Four different levels of care are available to CCRC residents. They include independent living, assisted living, skilled nursing care and memory support. For some, relocating to one of these facilities is based on need rather than on their choice. They are available according to the level of required care.[1]

These levels of care are described as follows.

INDEPENDENT LIVING

This kind of facility is geared towards active seniors leading healthy lives. They are represented by a variety of living facilities including single-family homes, condominiums, apartments and other multiple family dwellings. These retirement communities are not appreciably different from other residential communities around the country, except they have minimum age entry requirements. Residents lead active and challenging lives. The entry age is typically over fifty five years of age.

When an independent living retiree becomes sufficiently challenged to provide for his own personal care, and physical or mental health has sufficiently deteriorated, he is relocated to assisted living, skilled nursing or memory support. Decisions about moving are based on careful assessments.

ASSISTED LIVING

Assisted living facilities are primarily regulated and licensed at the state level. Some see such caregiving as a step in the wrong direction. These amenities are for individuals requiring assistance performing certain activities of daily living. This includes bathing, dressing, toiletry, and medication assistance. Patients' meals may be served in the community dining room. Other services can include housekeeping, transportation, exercise programs and recreational activities. This level of care falls between independent living and skilled nursing care.

As his condition becomes more challenged, the assisted living resident becomes a candidate for the skilled nursing

---

[1] For additional comments, consult Jane Mathis in *Home and Family Care*, June, 2012.

center. A higher level of personal physical or mental care is required.

SKILLED NURSING

A reader who is eager to learn more about skilled care facilities is referred to the Center for Medicare and Medicare Service's definition of skilled services for non-Medicaid and Medicare patients as stated in the Home Health Agency Manual, Sections 205.1 and 205.2. This is a complete source. In the meantime here is something more general.

Skilled nursing facilities provide care for life-limiting conditions on an around the clock basis. Treatment is based on a patient's need for care performed under the direction of a physician, nursing staff, physical and occupational therapists and social workers. Nursing care facilities care for more complex medical needs. They provide patient medical supplies. They are capable of administering drugs. They keep medical records. The facility has the capacity to develop wellness plans. The independent and assisted living sections of a CCRC cannot provide such a level of care.

MEMORY SUPPORT

These facilities care for patients who are unfortunate sufferers of Alzheimer's disease and other forms of dementia. In the earliest stages of this disability, a patient may be the resident of the independent or assisted living facility. When their mental state becomes more clearly compromised they are transferred from either lifestyle category to memory support. Eventually, as a patient's physical condition sufficiently worsens they can be transferred to the skilled nursing care facility.

Some residents will quietly say they would much rather continue living in assisted living than move to memory support. When you have difficulty remembering things it may not make a whole lot of difference.

The needed level of CCRC care is determined by personal health, the ability to cope, next of kin, facility management, and a physician. The elderly can take comfort in knowing that several options and levels of care are always available in a single CCRC location, which will meet their broadest needs.

MORE ABOUT CCRCs

Each year a growing number of the elderly enter the retirement community world. They are determined to live among the ranks of the survivors. They usually make wiser decisions about their futures after gaining more knowledge of the world of retirement community living.

It can be said that my CCRC is as descriptive of retirement communities as it is to say that the Heritage Hotel perfectly represents all properties of a national hotel chain. The hotel is somewhere back East. My place is on the West Coast.

Middle to upper income retirees have increasingly relocated to CCRCs, whose residents come from all walks of life. They typically relocate to this community life when living in the family home becomes too physically or mentally demanding.

Some CCRCs have quite hefty entrance fees and steep monthly dues. Potential customers are encouraged to explore creative move-in financing plans to facilitate admission. Marketing departments work to enhance the ability of retirees to select their facility. The family home may be a significant source of needed cash to facilitate relocating to the desired retirement. Poor real-estate market conditions can strain the capacity of some retirees to manage their up-front payment, and perhaps the monthly fees. As a consequence, temporary rentals and financial bridging arrangements are often discussed.

Stand-alone Assisted Living communities are an alternative retirement lifestyle to CCRC living. The former offer limited healthcare services. They charge a monthly fee, and no up-front residency payment is required. Both types of facilities are attractive to a growing number of baby boomers. An increasing number of retirees will spend the remainder of their retirement lives in either one of these communities. The majority will not regret their decision. A few may remain just as grumpy.

I once had to explain to a grandchild that I was not moving into an elderly folks' commune or a collective community. I said I was simply relocating to a community of elderly folks who planned to do their best to outlive each another. He believed me. I avoided mentioning that resident longevity can be detrimental to the cash-flow plans of community owners. We never did discuss the desired level of sensitivity to be demonstrated by community staffs towards residents' needs. Such topics can be too conceptual, except for the elderly.

In most retirement communities, male residents are in the minority. This is just a proclivity of nature. It was intended that way. Hence, we only have one pool table in my facility. Management would have installed another table if female residents thoroughly enjoyed playing pool.

My neighbor takes full advantage of this gender difference. He thrives on the opportunity to enjoy the dinner companionship of the more numerous female residents. They love him. He calls this the concealed social benefit of CCRC living.

The retirement community business is maturing. Older folks certainly believe that the United States Constitution is as thoughtful towards retirees as it is towards other citizens. It is ageless in its authority. The early days of American history showed no clear evidence of any comprehensive retirement community facilities. Back then the family home, the poor house, almshouses, boarding homes, hospices, or the street were options for the elderly and infirm. People died young. Medicare arrived many years after the untamed frontier had disappeared. We have all benefited from the pioneers who created this country.

In the past, the nation's families typically coped with their elderly relatives as best they were able. Families used self-directed catch-as-catch-can approaches to caregiving. Love filled their hearts. Over time society largely supported the steady fashioning of retirement community standards and approaches to meet obligations and necessities. Cost containment, quality of care, and resident satisfaction will remain vital keys to future caregiving. Government oversight and social advocacy will remain key aspects of the retiree environment.

There is no one best way to provide for retirement community living. Accommodations, contracts and terms vary. Alternative approaches to residential caregiving also vary, particularly for long-term assisted living and skilled nursing. Comparative advantage is a vital element in the marketplace.

Investors, promoters, and other corporate entities enter and exit the retirement care business. Community owners will make money while others lick their wounds. Some investors look enviously at their competitors, and new opportunities. Others will shy away from the vagaries of tending to the needs of cranky old retirees. The industry is not a transient hotel business. It is short or long-term care (indicating how long a resident will live) with an emphasis on sustained customer satisfaction and superior healthcare delivery. Cost management is a standard priority. The need by some community owners to stem an outflow of operating cash is a challenge. Change is inescapable.

Continued financial security and the ability to switch to a new lifestyle are important to new customers. Affordability, perceived value, retirement community features and benefits, as well as the quality of care received from an investment, are added considerations. Actuarial analyses, return on investment data, cost management programs, and marketing plans are of interest to the serious investor. On the other hand, resident satisfaction surveys may be of less importance.

Economic conditions can build pesky clouds that hang over the heads of prospective residents and community owners. This book does not compare and analyze retirement facility costs with value received. That is for another author.

"No Ms. Johnson, I said we need to cope, not to elope."

*"I never dared to be radical when young for fear it
would make me conservative when old."*
—Robert Frost

A STRONGHOLD OF RETIREMENT COMMUNITY SKEPTICISM

For a fleeting moment, when age was not a threatening factor in my life I developed the strong opinion that a retirement community might be a suitable place for me to rest my weary legs. I heard these places were uniquely suited for one's remaining years. I also wanted to fool my friends by dying laughing, or at least exciting, and with a smile. I was told these practices did not violate the residency rules of retirement communities. On the other hand, I wondered how a person could live on while slouched in a wheelchair in an understaffed nursing center. In spite of painstaking reflection, I found it difficult to reach a decision.

Anticipating further life on earth is important and to be encouraged. It can produce good feelings, even at the age of one hundred. However, I did not want to get excited about longevity in relation to a diminishing quality of life, and increasing dependency on caregivers.

Such random thoughts led me to several conclusions and decisions. I made an irrevocable pledge to avoid dying in any kind of hospital ward. Hopefully, fate would be on my side. I would be better served by dropping dead of a heart attack while watching a Dallas Cowboys football game. Unfortunately I no longer have Cowboys season tickets. Then again, I could move in with my kind daughter. An upshot of that might be the difficulty of several years of continuing medical annoyances while living in their home. At the same time, I would be competing with the family dog for their attention. I also real-ized that I wished to avoid dying in an ambulance that takes a wrong turn into a one-way street.

I tried to convince myself that I could miraculously devise a way to gain eternal retirement on earth. I rejected that idea since it might require a brain transplant or the need for some kind of cerebral mock-up, or patent protection. Patents ex-pire. So do some brain damaged individuals, which is a shame if they have just moved into a retirement facility.

At one point, I attempted to draw a solid distinction be-tween the various Laws of Life and their relationship to the Laws of the Universe and Human Consciousness. I then real-ized I was losing my senses, and any appreciation of reality. All this simply got me nowhere. I concluded that extremely elderly living might be dealt with in a more straightforward way. It occurred to me that simply reading more literature on retirement communities might not provide inescapable answers. In fact, such efforts might make things appear too easy.

The idea of living in a retirement community reoccurred to me. The thought of skilled nursing center living still bothered me. If these places were so skilled, why do so many people die in them? My next question was, "Why not die at home?" After all, I had diligently paid my property taxes. As I ruminated, it became clear there must be a more practical reasons for mov-ing into a soundly run retirement operation. I had friends who lived in one of these places. They all seemed happy, and con-tinued to talk politely to each another.

I decided to more thoroughly investigate my options. My first choice was to research a retirement community that nev-er served salty food, never showed signs of regimentation, never showed weekend movies and did not have any exercise bikes. I came up empty-handed.

Someone then suggested I look for a community that showed appreciable empathy towards its residents, offered personal security, had unusually caring employees, good food, companionship, and offered peaceful living. I came up with hundreds of listings. They were all prepared to satisfy my needs.

Somewhere out there was a suitable facility for me. Might I find other retirement living modes for myself? Especially should my stay in their nursing center proved to be a long one.

During my search for senior citizen bliss, I talked to a pleasant retirement community salesperson. He guaranteed I would age more gradually while living in his retirement facility. He said I would also age gracefully. I was unsure what he intended by that. Maybe he meant I would survive in his place until I reached 105 years in age, and that I would never lose my sweet smile.

A period of more gradual aging appealed to me. So much so that my concern about salty food and nursing care centers utterly vanished. In fact, if they guaranteed the "extremely slow aging" feature I would enthusiastically eat all the salty food their chef could serve me. I now tend to over-salt my food.

A PANORAMA OF RETIREMENT COMMUNITIES

The narratives included in *Here Today and Perhaps Tomorrow* go beyond describing the bricks and mortar of a retirement community. They intend to convey a clearer understanding of certain intimacies and relationships that envelop the residents of a community. A few elderly residents unfairly think they live in some form of supervised custody. They do not. The book provides a closer feeling for the sedate, and even edgy sides of retirement facilities. It also describes certain influences that shape the character of such places.

I can only vouch for the daytime incidents in a retirement community, and make no attempt to describe what happens at night. This would require a book on rejuvenation.

The book was not written to intimidate a seventy-eight-year-old youngster facing a significant and upcoming lifestyle transition. Neither was it written to explain why some challenged folks criticize others, are always smiling, or why some elderly folks keep wetting their pants.

My own community enjoys sunny weather and close-by shopping. It is well organized. Both residents and staff are very helpful. Scheduled activities are abundant. Management can take much credit for the planning and organizing that contribute to operating success. After all, they granted all their residents permission to move into the facility. Nostalgia exists. Family visits are planned and enjoyed. We are rarely visited by ex-girlfriends, or ex-boyfriends.

Decisions about moving into retirement communities are quite subjective, even after the investigation is completed. We all know full well that my place is better than your place. My apartment has a far better view than yours does. Why are we better here? Well, we have a large swimming pool. The pool water temperature is always kept reasonably warm. We are locally known as the place where residents can depend on lukewarm water in the swimming pool.

Grandchildren enjoy their visits here and rave about the food. This might not say a whole lot about home cooking. Their comments may be caused by their access to the downstairs pool table, and the ice cream served upstairs. I rarely do my dishes and remind my relatives of that. They react in awe.

Empty apartments are always available in many communities. Management lays down new carpeting and applies a coat of fresh paint prior to a new resident moving in. This practice stimulates apartment sales. You need to explore other move-in deals.

Complimentary breakfasts are served each morning. If community costs keep increasing this retiree benefit may receive serious management scrutiny. Diminishing breakfast service will never happen. It might trigger a revolt. You need to find out what characterizes elderly revolts.

You may want to do more trolling in the retirement marketplace before you finally decide to move in. The pivotal moment is when you roll the dice and make your apartment selection decision. Your creaking body will be pleased when you decide to go for it. Living in my facility has provided convenience, security, and pleasure. Would I do it again? I probably would. Alternatives are not limitless. The elderly have fewer options as they age. When a retiree gets very old, he may barely remember that nasty next door neighbor in Joliet, Illinois who made such a confounded ruckus all the time. We become increasingly aware that memory loss makes for greater forgetfulness.

GAPS BETWEEN EXPECTATIONS AND REALITY

When visiting a retirement community, the adventuresome and curious appreciate an opportunity to learn about the joys of retirement living. This may thwart any pessimism about relocating to an uncertain new world. Some individuals seeking retirement community information may prefer to use the Internet to find helpful answers to questions. This is encouraged.

Retirement residences are like social clubs that allow their managements to create all kinds of social rules and restrictions. **Here Today and Perhaps Tomorrow** introduces you to club living.

If you have an interest in visiting a retirement community, contact one and request an inspection. A prospective purchaser should feel comfortable about asking a marketing department to extend an invitation to stay overnight. This will allow the curious to better appreciate a facility and make an educated decision about possibly moving in, or to look elsewhere. Most existing residents you meet will emphasize the qualities of the magnificent facility they occupy. They are usually right. An occasional resident will mumble something in your ear.

Residents that you chat with may avoid revealing too much local scuttlebutt, political persuasions, or religious convictions. These are dubbed serious subjects that remain taboo unless you all attend the same temple, or belong to the Democratic Party. Residents will inevitably assess visitors, and typically avoid reporting their impressions about you to the staff. Hosts do find out what kind of lipstick you wear, what your hobbies are, and where you met your third wife. Visitors may catch a retirement community joke or two. For instance.

"Edgar, I have a leak!"
"In your apartment or is it your bladder?" asked the maintenance man.

You must laugh loudly at such jokes. They quickly make the rounds.

Do not expect anyone to reel off exciting news about their community. Someone may ask you if you heard those screaming sirens during the night. They will explain that two ambulances departed from the nursing center last evening at extremely high speed. They are now checking on who the occupants were.

Talk things over while you return home. Consult with your dog. He must also qualify to move in with you. Dogs weighing over 25 pounds (including their collars) are infrequently accepted by community managements. Dogs are never told they cannot have the run of the facility.

"You keep forgetting dear, another strict rule here
is we have to dress for dinner."

WORDS OF CAUTION FOR CCRC PROSPECTS

New residents may not appreciate the problem of finding new doctors and friends. Having settled down a new resident may decide he will never again cook food in his apartments, unless he decides to check out the fire-alarm system. There is sadness in having to downsize to a smaller living area. Fitting large furniture into a small apartment is a significant task. A minimum requirement is one comfortable bed.

Residents occasionally get to ride a retirement community bus to symphony concerts. Another benefit is that this bus will drop residents off in front of the Symphony Hall. A word of caution to bus riders. Never sit in the back of a retirement community bus, unless you need a herniated disk. Residents are also advised never to sleep on the floor of their apartments unless they need to relieve their herniated disk.

Fear of being transferred to assisted living or the skilled nursing center impels an occasional resident to work day and night on his exercise bike. This thrilling experience fails to exercise the mind. It makes one strong in the leg and weak in the head. An all-night physical therapy center might improve things.

FAMILY SUPPORT AND ELDERLY VALUES

We have come a long way since society and local custom loosened a concept that the family unit has a strong responsibility to care for elderly kin. American family members are increasingly dispersed around this country. Cultural values pertaining to the elderly have shifted. The retirement community business was eventually born and blossomed. My father and mother rarely mentioned retirement communities. They sometimes mentioned "old folk's homes," which they reacted to with skepticism.

Consider the ways in which an evolving Chinese society might address elderly living in relation to family mobility trends, family caregiving ideals, intentions, and societal pressures. All these will undoubtedly be influenced by China's shifting family norms and values. Regardless, the dining rooms of their new found retirement communities will gladly serve extra-large portions of noodles.

WHY AM I LIVING HERE?

A much bandied existential question is, "Why am I here?" Adding the word "living" to this question makes it more relevant. It meshes better with the scope of this book. Perhaps cultural and social diversities are the reasons for residing in a CCRC. Maybe it is the swimming pool, community location, or the food. It might be because a resident can ambitiously get elected to a leadership position representing the other inhabitants. Resident leadership elections sometimes cause noteworthy community commotion. Councils and committees are integral parts of many communities. Why not get personally involved in community affairs? It might be a way to get more friends. It could become an easier way to make enemies, thus forcing you to reflect on another question "What am I doing here?"

Some retirement community residents own beautifully shampooed dogs. Their pets appreciate a comfortable vantage point when riding on their owners' scooters. They can be spoiled rotten. This does not solve the question of "Why I am here?" The short answer is that I appreciate retirement community living. I feel management will provide quality health care. Also, that the living environment is of sufficient value to justify the investment and monthly dues. I like my independence. I trust the owners.

Some residents hesitated to play the stock market until they joined an in-house investment club. They now accept the advice of a retired old stockbroker who was born during the Great Depression. As in other retirement communities it all comes down to trust. Trust investment advisors who recall the Great Depression. Trust executives who are committed to hosting you in their retirement community.

HERE TODAY AND PERHAPS TOMORROW HAVE CONSEQUENCES

Satire is an ancient technique that can add to a message. Perhaps not so in the statistical area. This book offers few statistics. It contains many old folks' tales. Statistical information is to be avoided when people are referred to by a numbers. Unpopular numbers turn up when resident mortality data or relocations to the nursing center are discussed.

The writer wishes to create impressions rather than ply the reader with theory. If a statement has an impractical ring, the implicit message does not. Here are some points to consider as you continue reading.

- If you become skeptical, you obviously do not have a grandparent living in a CCRC.
- If you do not giggle a time or two, avoid reading a serious book about retirement community living.
- If you feel badly at some point in your reading you may not live long enough to enjoy life in a retirement facility.
- If you sometimes feel sad about the elderly, you will eventually feel glad in a retirement community.
- If you think this book is a deliberate exaggeration, you have not lived in one of these facilities.

Some examples of pertinent questions commonly asked about retirement communities.

"What goes on in there?"
"What's their food like?"
"How well do they treat you?"
"Are you happy there?"
"Why didn't we move in earlier?"
"Does the staff really run a funny farm?"

During limited encounters with retirement facilities, a visitor or prospective purchaser might only gain a broad understanding of retirement community living. This limitation may still apply after reading the literature, surfing the Internet and been wined and dined. Impressions and decisions might be based on biased information. The sales pitch may have been exaggerated, or your judgment was faulty. After all, you sometimes hear what you want to hear.

When all is said and done, a prospective CCRC customer may feel he bought into the wrong place. Alternatively, renting a property might have been a sounder decision. The retirement community lifestyle is not for everyone. Apartment selection, meal plans, and car parking decisions should only be made after an individual agrees that the CCRC concept can become a part of his life. An important consideration is being obliged to live with umpteen other elderly residents, all of whom are as choosy as you can be.

"Someday you will be old enough to start reading fairy tales again."
—C. S. Lewis

CHAPTER FOUR

A MEDLEY OF VIGNETTES, ANECDOTES AND SERIOUS NARRATIVES

COMMITMENT - CONTENTMENT - COMPASSION - COMMOTION

Chapter Four describes social sceneries associated with retirement community living. It does not single out a particular community. This Chapter is divided into nine parts. Each contains stories and settings about continuing care retirement communities. Portraits are painted of the retirement world. Stories include topics such as social interactions, skilled and other caregiving centers, interfaces with public organizations, the residents themselves, and the management of retirement communities.

This Chapter generates a broad picture of retiree *'Commitment, Contentment, Compassion and Commotion'* in communities across our country. The scenarios are portrayed by means of images about this environment. Some are more detailed than others. They are presented in anecdotal as well as serious narrative styles. They are grouped according to theme.

Some narratives are lighthearted or softhearted. An example or two ends up being slightly irreverent. Some admonish. Two narratives look at institutional and governmental affairs. They attempt to describe real-life situations, images, and influences. One Section reflects on the quality of skilled nursing care around the country.

The Chapter can be funny, sad, provocative, challenging, and full of pathos and bathos. It captures the liveliness, challenges, dynamics, and tensions of retirees and retirement care. The narratives portray a retirement odyssey. Some look within and beyond retirement communities and reflect on the fact that old folks are so dependent on medical care, nursing centers, acupuncture, buying flowers, gambling, and getting their toenails pedicured.

Chapter Four is divided into nine Parts. They are outlined as follows.

Part I.   **The Caring Side of Continuing Care Retirement Communities.**
This Part offers a candid exploration of retirement community residency, and is sincere in its content. Tedium may be an acceptable obstacle to leading a lively community life. Retirement life can be funny and sometimes sad. Residents' feelings can be arbitrary or frivolous.

Part II.   **A Potpourri of Retiree Conversations and Attitudes.**
The conversations presented here are sometimes out of the ordinary, engagingly candid, mundane, or emotional. They reflect attitudes and feelings.

Part III. **Resident Health and Wellness.**
Healthcare and coping can be the centerpiece of retiree conversations. This may lead to critical

thinking about how to fix the state of one's mind and body. This Part looks at the importance of healthcare discussions in many retirees' lives. Sadly eternity may be just around the corner. To my knowledge retirement communities do not operate in eternity.

Part IV. **Managing Retirement Communities.**
This is an attempt to prove that all retirement communities have faultless managing directors and resident-friendly community policies. Part IV deals with managing retirement communities. It recognizes that the elderly field can require as much orderliness and direction as is required of a teenage son. It also recognizes that communities must operate within budgets and comply with policies. It brings to mind that management must skillfully adhere to healthcare laws, and the intents of corporate ownership. Communities are invariably managed by caring staffs that have the welfare of the of the elderly at heart. This Part does assume that managers always make the right decisions.

Part V. **Legislation, Lobbying and Retirement Communities.**
A reminder that politics and advocacy play key roles in a retirement living environment. Government agencies and lobbyists have played an important role in advocating on behalf of CCRC residents. After all, residents have committed hard-earned savings to enjoy retirement community occupancy. They are exposed to the vagaries of complex ownership issues and strategic financial options. Government entities have a background of protecting retiree interests.

Part VI. **Continuing Care Retirement Communities and Skilled Nursing.**

Skilled nursing centers play a vital and integral role in continuing care retirement communities. They can involve crucial short and long periods of residency, especially for recuperative and palliative care for the seriously afflicted. The next level up is a hospital. Nursing care staffs also find this environment challenging and demanding. Standards of care delivery must be high. The sick are so very dependent on the extent and the quality of caregiving they receive. The author's emphasis on this facet of CCRC care permits a more detailed analysis of a particularly important aspect of retirement community caregiving.

Part VII. **Retiree Happenings in the Outside World.**

Why do those entities do these things to us? Part VII provides examples of the irritations and inconveniences retirees periodically experience while they interact with the outside world. The medical profession receives some attention. At times some consumer industry practices do annoy the retiree.

Part VIII. **Personal Feelings about Retirement Community Living.**

This Part is not a definitive analysis. It does not advise individuals about relocating to a specific retirement community. Neither does it prove that I am a bizarre or compulsive retiree. It includes a subjective assessment of various aspects of retirement community living. It avoids being definitive and may even be inaccurate. It makes no effort to advise individuals on making decisions about their financial affairs. It lists some subjective biases, values and feelings.

Part IX. Romance and Retirement Communities.
This Part requires little elaboration. Love does conquer all.

Chapter Five brings to life many aspects of retirement community living. *Here Today and Perhaps Tomorrow* does not tattle on seniors. It simply wishes to inform the reader about some goings on, such as the resident who from time to time removes a dinner roll or two from the dining room after eating his dinner. Actually, this snitching is noteworthy. Some say this behavior is just rumor. Retirees who underestimate this dinner roll report are probably the very ones who remove the baked goods. I prefer to place an occasional potato in my pants pocket. It must not be too large or too hot. A baked potato is less messy.

Perhaps the contents of this book far exceed the creativity of any retirement community's marketing brochures, or advertising. My information is as relevant to retirees as many promotional materials.

"The universe is made of stories, not atoms."
—*Muriel Rukeyser*

PART I
THE CARING SIDE OF CONTINUING CARE RETIREMENT COMMUNITIES

AN OLD MAN LIVES ON

Old age and retirement communities are cut from the same cloth. This story has a somber note. It relates to an old man living in a skilled nursing center. The tale is rather sad. After all, retirement living can have more than its share of sadness. Part One of the book begins like this because skilled nursing facilities may eventually play a very prominent role in an individual's CCRC experience. This vignette helps character-ize a facet of skilled care life in such a community.

Retirement living has its ups and downs. Happiness and pleasures gladden us. Somber feelings affect us. Growing very old triggers more serious health issues. Most of us learn to cope in our own ways.

An old man is in the waning years of his life. The story begins . . . .

The patient was bedridden in a skilled nursing facility. He was old but not considered to be extremely old, which any observant retiree might have guessed. Some retirees tell you that old people are extremely old after they exceed ninety-five years of age. He was ninety one, so he had not yet arrived. Others will say it was providential he was alive and had managed so nicely in spite of it all. Some were less surprised and said luck was on his side, and that he should already have hopped into heaven. The prevailing notion was that his time had not arrived. You need to realize that extremely old folks are particularly averse to further aging.

It was early morning, and the sun began to shine into room 604. The nursing center was still quiet. It verged on full daytime activities. Residents had not yet made their early morning trips to the bathroom. Bathroom visits were a sign that things will soon pick up and that the normal daytime rhythm would soon get underway. Trips to the bathroom presaged visits to the dining room. Always in that order. It was light outside and a new day. The dispensers of health care were about to change shifts.

When he elevated his head from his pillow, and stared beyond his bedroom window, he could stare at the retirement apartment he had occupied with his wife for several years. It was on the 11th floor of the adjacent tall building. His eyesight had deteriorated. Nonetheless, he always recognized the windows of the apartment he and his wife had called home. That was a time when the community staff categorized both of them as "active retirement" residents. He was now a "nursing center resident." This did not seem to be any kind of promotion. He laughed when his wife referred to him as an "inactive retirement resident". The staff simply said he was a courteous old gentleman.

He often reflected on the apartment they had shared behind those windows. They lived there in quiet privacy. It was exceptionally comfortable. Numerous artifacts were displayed which they collected locally and abroad during many years of travel. Someone said the place had the appearance of a museum. Over time, they enjoyed undisturbed security and experienced a truly home-style life. They got along with most residents. Friendships were easily made.

They did their best to stay active, and took frequent trips around the country, which often included family visits. Their daily routine involved grocery shopping, attending the symphony, picking up prescriptions at the pharmacy, reading books, and playing golf.

Both appreciated the housekeeper who cleaned their apartment. Because of her foreign accent they sometimes found her a little difficult to understand. He enjoyed many community-organized lectures but never attended any pertaining to retirement living. This topic reminded him that he lived in a retirement community that might eventually classify him as an "inactive resident."

Almost ten years of living in that high-rise building were noteworthy. Living over there seemed like a long time ago. Yes, he was now a patient in the skilled nursing center. His wife continued to live in the apartment beyond his window. They remained constant companions, which is why his gaze wondered over there so often. She visited him every day. They chatted while she held his hand. Never again would she say to him, "You'll certainly pay for that." That was back in those days.

He was not a stranger to the care center. Over a year had gone by since he had relocated from their apartment. That seemed like an unusually long time for anyone to occupy a bed across from the tall building. To be exact, he had relocated 547 days ago. The old man again reckoned by the day. He was a military veteran who had likewise counted his World War Two service days.

Patients moved to the center to recuperate from surgery, or other serious health reasons. Such residents typically returned home after a stay of about seven days to two weeks. Not him. He knew he had a one-way non-refundable ticket.

From time to time, he dearly wished he could go back to that apartment and rejoin his wife. That was not to be. They said he would remain in the care center indefinitely, which was unpleasant to hear. It was explained in a kindly way. The old man accepted it graciously.

They had wheeled him into room 604. A few cherished belongings accompanied him. His wife hung some of them on the walls or placed them on his nightstand. Each was a pleasant reminder of the past.

That early morning he was jarred into reality by a day-shift LVN who entered his room and greeted him.

"Good morning, sir. How are you? Did you sleep well?"
"Well, thank you, very well," he replied. "What day is it?"
"It's Thursday. That's the day we give you your shower, isn't it?" she replied.
"Yes," he responded.
"Here's your medicine, be sure to drink lots of water."
He swallowed both and watched her leave the room.
Later, the center's social director walked in and greeted him.
"Would you like to take a bus ride today along with some other residents?" she asked.
The driver is taking a group to Brittany Park to see the swans."
"That's nice," he said. "Yes, I'd like to go. Can we feed them?" he asked.
"Yes you can," she replied.
She left his room.
A little later Dr. Maxwell walked in.
They greeted each another. The doctor moved to his bedside and smiled.

"Good morning, sir. You look well," the doctor exclaimed.

"Good morning, Doctor," he replied.

The doctor said to him, "We have good news for you. The X-ray of your chest came back negative. You'll live to be a hundred."

"Then may I return to my apartment?"

"Not today. We need to keep you here for a few more days," replied the doctor.

"That's what you told me last year," he responded.

The doctor left his room.

An aide carried in his breakfast tray.

"Where would you like me to put your tray?" she asked.

"The same old place," he replied.

"Do you want your food cut up?"

"Yes, please, into little pieces. Leave the coffee close to my tray."

She cut the food up into small pieces.

"Please, eat it all," she commented as she left.

The nursing facility was now alive. This was a new day with fresh experiences to greet each of the sixty-two other care center residents. A few occupants planned to check out today. Other residents would remain a few more days. A few residents would be less fortunate. For them, another bus trip would again compete with their television sets.

He felt he needed to void, so he pushed his call button. An aide entered the room. "Please, help me get to the bathroom. I'm leaking," he said. It hurt when he voided. Yes, the Care Center was back to its daily routine.

A CLOSELY GUARDED SENIOR HEALTHCARE SECRET

The tales continue with a lighthearted story about another very elderly gentleman. It suggests that integrity is as complicated in a healthcare-conscious environment as it is beyond these premises. The following situation does not strictly describe typical resident behaviors as they experience a need for care. Residents' intentions vary as they go about coping with life's needs.

He resides in the active retirement part of his community. He is a normal person of sound mind but perhaps not of body. He is elderly and fragile. If you do not believe this ask the nurse.

Sometimes he attempts to compare his own community with the seven other retirement facilities in town. He ends up concluding that their lawns are just as well manicured. They all charge less.

Each year they ask him to take an Alzheimer's memory test which he always passes so easily. Why is he capable of answering the standard test questions without any difficulty? Before taking the test, he writes down the correct answer to each question on the palm of one hand. He also keeps both hands under the table. The nurse does not test his palms. Neither does she look under the table.

He also plays this deception game with the pencil drawing he is subsequently asked to draw. The picture he carefully sketches on a piece of paper during the test is always wrinkly. Just like what he had drawn on his other palm.

After taking the test, he hesitates to wash his hands to avoid removing all that valuable information. His friends died laughing when he mentions this escapade to them. He once thought about preserving the information on each hand until the test is repeated the following year.

Some folks do not pass the Alzheimer's test. This can be distressing. Failing the test is a sign they may be headed to the memory support unit. Someone once said that staying in a memory support facility is like serving time in a brig. This is absolutely untrue. The memory support facility receives anguished visitors who show compassion and caring. You can say the same thing about brigs. This is simply mystified thinking.

"The problem with me Amy is that I forget
what I didn't remember the day before."

RESEARCHING A RETIREMENT FACILITY THAT FITS YOUR NEEDS

An elderly couple decided to comprehensively research continuing care retirement communities. Their intent was to relocate to the preferred facility that would meet their needs. The task began by devising a sophisticated market research model. The planning phase took three months. It took them one year to complete their field work. Their friends were impressed. Someone asked them whether they employed blasé business survey tools for their field work. They smugly answered all those technical questions.

Work on finding a retirement community must extend beyond finding opportunities for the retiree to socialize and make many friends. The following is a basic technique designed to collect CCRC information. It employs a diagnostic approach and contains many questions to be asked while visiting retirement facilities. They include many key features and benefits of these retirement communities.

FACILITY LOCATION

1. Should we retire in the United States or overseas?
2. What geographic areas are preferred?
3. What kind of local climate is preferred?
4. Do we want to retire in a small town, the suburbs, or in a city?
5. Do we want to locate near a shopping center?
6. Do we want to be near entertainment?

7. Is the facility near churches or a synagogue?
8. Is the facility near a library?
9. Is there a golf course nearby?
10. Do we want to locate near the ocean, the mountains, or away from a fault line?
11. Is it in a quiet neighborhood?

MEDICAL

12. What medical facilities are located nearby?
13. Are local medicals/therapeutic services sufficiently reliable?
14. Do they provide complimentary transportation service to or from medical facilities?
15. Is prompt ambulance service available?
16. What standards are enforced in the skilled nursing facility?
17. Do they have a support nurse center?
18. Do they provide in-house physical/occupational therapy services?
19. Single or double rooms on the nursing center?

PUBLIC TRANSPORTATION

20. What public transportation is available?
21. Is the facility close to expressways, a park?

PUBLIC SAFETY

22. Is there a fire station nearby?
23. Is there adequate police surveillance in the area?

THE FACILITY

24. Do we prefer a liquor licensed community?
25. Do we prefer a high- or low-rise building?

26. Are there elevators?
27. Is there a nurse care center?
28. Are we primarily looking for independent living, assisted living, skilled nursing, or memory support? Or all four?
29. What rating do we give each facility?
30. Do we prefer for-profit or not-for-profit facilities?
31. Do we prefer a secular residency, or a church sponsored one?
32. Do we prefer a large chain, or a stand-alone independent facility?
33. What are the apartment sizes and layouts?
34. Are the facilities well cared for?
35. Are the property owners in strong financial shape?
36. Is their car parking under cover?
37. How secure might we feel?

FACILITY SERVICES

38. What kind of recreational and social activities are offered, such as a "happy hour?"
39. What are the dining hours?
40. What kind of food and dining services are offered?
41. What exercise programs are provided? By whom?
42. Do their activities include interesting lecture series, movies, etc?
43. Did marketing satisfactorily respond to our financial questions?
44. What is the tipping procedure?
45. Do they provide carry-up service for groceries/heavy items? from the entryway to apartments?
46. What facility transportation services are there?
47. What pet restrictions do they have?

FACILITY SECURITY

48. What is the facility's security plan? Fire, etc.?
49. What is the size of the security staff?

THE RESIDENTS

50. Did we enjoy the folks we met when we visited?
51. What is the entry age?
52. What is the age spread of the residents?
53. Did we enjoy the ambiance there?

THE STAFF

54. Is there a caring feeling there?
55. Does the staff seem to be professional?
56. Do they appear organized?
57. Were they responsive to inquiries/questions?

THE PROPERTY PRICE AND MONTHLY COSTS

58. What residency options do we now have?
59. What discounts and deals do they offer?
60. What is the up-front cost?
61. What is the monthly fee?
62. What is the history of monthly fee increases?
63. What unit(s) can we afford?
64. Nonrefundable/refundable unit price? How much?
65. What refundable down payment plans do they offer? What percentages?
66. Should we opt for a monthly rental property with no down payment?
67. Other?

The research theory couple decided not to ask if any of the retirement communities visited were sufficiently near to a cemetery.

The couple applied their criteria to the twenty-five retirement facilities they visited during their coast-to-coast saga. They traveled to twelve states. They spent fifteen nights in eighteen different communities. They each drank eighteen martinis as part of various well-geared and subtle marketing pitches. They enjoyed complimentary dinners with thirty-seven community residents. They patted five small dogs belonging to various residents, and filled five notebooks with data.

They eventually concluded the perfect place for them to move to was located eighteen miles from where they now lived. Their decision was never mentioning to anyone. The researchers still brag about their extensive travel and sophisticated strategy.

An implication of this narrative is that there is no need to produce segmented marketing data to help find a preferred retirement community. Reading the literature, talking to others, making phone calls, surfing the internet and personal visits are all successful approaches to productive decision making. The key is asking relevant questions. On the other hand, some retirees simply end up living right alongside old friends who had already relocated to a retirement community. Friends can be an excellent source of retirement information and companionship.

"I particularly like their nursing facility."

ANNOUNCING THE ARRIVAL OF FOUR NEW RESIDENTS

Retirement communities face unending resident turnover. Younger residents replace the old. The following community bulletin confirms that new arrivals come from all walks of life.

THE TALLEST TIMBERS RETIREMENT COMMUNITY

August 18th.

To all residents,

We are pleased to welcome four new residents who joined us last week. The following is background information on these newcomers.

Mr. Sol. Baruch was born in Berlin, Germany. He completed preparatory school and planned to attend a local university. Mr. Baruch was able to avoid Nazi concentration camps. He eventually escaped from Germany and traveled by a circuitous route to Spain, where he lived for seven months. He subsequently obtained a visa to enter Swaziland in Southern Africa. He lived there for five years, until the end of WWII. At the end of the war, he found a sponsor for admission to the United States. He relocated to New York City.

Roger Swanson and his wife Mary were both born in Birmingham, AL, where they both received their high-school educations. He received a scholarship to attend MIT where he eventually received his Ph.D. His area of specialization was nuclear physics. Dr. Swanson initially taught at U.C. Berkeley. He was subsequently employed by the Atomic Energy Commission and worked at their National Laboratory in Los Alamos, NM. He played a prominent role in the further development of our nuclear arsenal. They have moved here from New Mexico.

Ms. Elsa Jenkins was married to Roger Jenkins, now deceased. They were married for 56 years. She attended high school in Perrysburg, OH and received a B.A. in history from Bowling Green State University. Upon graduation, she married Mr. Jenkins. She enjoyed being a devoted homemaker and mother. They had five children, seventeen grandchildren, and one great grandchild.

Please join us in welcoming these four residents to our community.

Sylvia Johnson

Marketing Department

A LETTER TO THE ATTORNEY GENERAL OF THE UNITED STATES

The following is an important and self-explanatory letter that was circulated at high levels within the United States Department of Justice.

MOST CONFIDENTIAL

September 9.

Dear Attorney General Smithson,

We wish to notify the Attorney General that Mr. Roberto R. Bollini, Sr., was until recently a longtime participant in the Federal Witness Protection Program. He died on July 21.

For his safety, the FBI had placed Mr. Bollini in a large retirement community in Colorado. This relocation occurred over six years ago. He was very well cared for throughout his stay. We were occasionally informed he conducted himself appropriately. The Department should note that the cost of his residency to the United States Government was unexpectedly high.

A retirement community venue for elderly individuals needing Witness Protection makes excellent sense. Opportunities to expand the Program need to be reviewed. We believe that other elderly individuals requiring enrollment in our Protection Program would benefit by being assigned by us to such communities. A cap of one individual per community is advisable. We recommend conducting a survey to identify other U.S. facilities for inclusion in the Department's Program. It is interesting to note that Mr. Bollini blended well into his residency. At one time, he served as Chair of their Resident Activities Committee. A notable strength was his ability to manage their social agenda.

We will contact the FBI and suggest they make an effort to place another Federal Witness Protection Program nominee into this Colorado community. The Bureau has done an excellent job. A high level of confidentiality must be maintained to protect this valuable Program for the elderly.

Sincerely,

William Stanson

William Stanson,
United States District Attorney, Denver, CO

If you check with the residents of an eastern retirement community, you will discover they are more than eager to designate a resident for a different kind of protection program.

WELL ORGANIZED ACTIVITIES DO KEEP RETIREES BUSY

R eading the following daily activities schedule indicates that retirement communities are truly landlocked cruise ships.

THE EMBERS AT PLACID LAKE

The Daily Schedule for Thursday, June 4th

8:15	FLEXIBILITY AND FITNESS
9:00	CARDIO CLASS
9:15	SENIOR FITNESS
10:00	DEEP BREATHING, RELAXATION & ACUPUNCTURE
10:00	PLAY READING
10:30	NEEDLE CRAFTERS
1:30	COFFEE, TEA AND COOKIES
2:00	BUS TRIP TO THE SHOPPING CENTER*
2:30	LECTURE: EDWARD REESE, PH.D., PROFESSOR OF FINE ART, EISU: "THE SCULPTURES OF AUGUSTE RODIN"
3:00	SOCIAL BRIDGE
4:00	COMPUTER SUPPORT CLUB
7:00	BINGO
7:15	MOVIE: " THE GREAT ESCAPE"

HAPPY BIRTHDAY, FRED YOUNG AND CLAIRE SOKOL!

* You must sign up for the bus trip.

A CAPRICIOUS WAY TO STEREOTYPE A RESIDENT

Who knows not, and knows not that he knows not, is foolish; shun him.
Who knows not, and knows that he knows not, is humble; teach him.
Who knows, but knows not that he knows, is asleep; wake him.
Who knows, and knows that he knows, is wise; follow him.
Follow Him! For not only is He wise. He is Wisdom itself.
—A wise ancient

Continuing care retirement communities have unique cultures and individualities. Residents have their individual differences and distinct personalities. They contain irritable old men and sweet old ladies, and vice versa. Wide ranging dispositions occasionally cause mayhem in a community. The common denominator is living together and getting along. We do our best to avoid repeating random impulses.

Some individuals form social cliques that affirm or reinforce their affinity for a particular trait, social grouping or religion. Some groups have the audacity to feel superior. One of management's visionary goals is to assemble a gathering of community residents to form a team, comparable to elderly football. Bridge groups are evidence of competitive togetherness. This circle of players may not appeal to a serious golfer, who might attract his own circle of friends.

In addition, there is the relationship between management and residents. This interaction is influenced by their diverse personalities. The extent of their harmony is evidenced by such behaviors as battling to the courthouse steps, or harmoniously agreeing on the disposal of trash. Marketing brochures neglect to disclose such events. They present pictures of a thriving residential community with friendly and caring relationships.

Residents usually enter the portals of a retirement community with the highest curiosity about the people they will meet, and how they will interact with others. Successfully judging and assessing themselves and others in this new environment can be challenging. This is otherwise known as adjusting and making friends.

To help the individual better cope with his integration it may be useful to look at several personality types that coexist in a community. They are randomly identified here and are non-specific in nature. Studying these types too intensely produces anxiety or unease. It can lay the ground for subversive retiree behavior, which has yet to be clearly described for retirement communities.

Arbitrary examples of four contrasting personality types are listed below. A trained assessor will end up branding this classification process as significantly illogical. Others may suggest it will cause trouble. To be called a troublemaker is a desperate attempt by some to create an additional personality type. The troublemaker label is rarely applied among friends.

The **JOINER** type.

> They join everything, want more involvement, expect more, and feel badly when others turn them down. They promote affiliation.

The **RESERVED** type.

> They may keep to themselves and be more independent. Life just happens to these people. They can be shy and quiet.

The **INTERVENTIONIST** type.

> They are contentious. They want to run things or be in full command. They can be movers and shakers. They might be opinionated and complainers.

The **BALANCED** type.

> Truly magnificent people. Folks who bind together and introduce sound logic when the community wobbles. These folks are flexible, open, and friendly.

Everybody wants to be seen as a "Balanced Type."

Another behavioral type may be characterized by the words "Don't get mad, get even!" The presence of this type has serious consequences in a community. You do not want these individuals around. After all, enough is enough at age eighty six.

A BEAUTY CONTEST FOR DOGS

A group of residents suggested a retirement community organize a beauty contest for the residents' dogs. The idea was warmly received by the well groomed dogs.

A contest committee was appointed. The committee members prepared program publicity, agreed on the contestant categories and selected the judges.

Community management provided the dog prizes.

Event planning proceeded remarkably well.

The contest moved into the final stretch.

At the last minute, the committee chairperson announced that a contest prize would be awarded to

THE DOG THAT LOOKED MOST LIKE ITS OWNER!

A last minute announcement was made that prizes would be awarded to both the dog and its owner.

This was a terrible move. The dogs strenuously objected. The community's carpets began to take the brunt of their objections.

The retirement community never considered another dog beauty contest.

DEVELOPING COMPUTER SKILLS

There are ongoing and persistent attempts to help community residents become more knowledgeable about their computers and software programs. This also includes efforts to improve the technical skills of experienced computer owners. The following edited bulletin was circulated by the chair of a community's Resident Computer Group.[2]

---

[2] Computer Group Information Bulletin. With permission.

THE COMPUTER GROUP

Dear Resident,

Attention all you computer buffs—and those who would like to be! Did you know we have a very active Computer Group here? This group is one of our longest-running resident activities. It came into being some fifteen years ago when some residents began to informally get together to share their computer knowledge, experiences, and problems.

Helping residents learn about computer usage and software programs has always been our main objective. The group serves PC, Mac and iPad users. Over the years, both outside speakers and knowledgeable residents have provided valuable programs. When new operating systems and new software are available, arrangements are made to have someone come in and talk about them. For example, a manager from a software products company recently introduced new software. Outside classes are sometimes available. The group encourages residents to take advantage of these programs. Teachers have been invited to conduct in-house classes. The group plans to include question-and-answer sessions at future meetings.

The Computer Group has also set up resources to help any resident who has a computer problem. In addition, some resident computer experts will occasionally make house calls!

Check our website for more information. Click on "Computer Group Events, News, and Resources." You will find announcements of Computer Group meetings, other events, articles on hardware and software, and a list of the residents' email addresses.

REGULAR MONTHLY MEETING SCHEDULE

The General Computer Group meets on the 3rd Thursday of every month at 11:00 am in the Laurel Room. We are available to give basic computer support services every Saturday of the month at 1:00 pm, also in the Laurel Room.

RESIDENT DISINTEREST IN THE INTERNET

An important part of any traditional skills training efforts is the use of learned knowledge in the workplace. In this case, the retirement community facility. This approach can work very well, and skills are improved. Occasionally, newly learned skills simply remain dormant.

The following staff memorandum demonstrates an attempt by management to get residents to apply their newly learned computer knowledge back in their community.

MEMORANDUM

August 15th.

To: All residents

From: Jill Revere, Director of Services

Subject: <u>ANNOUNCEMENTS VIA EMAIL</u>

There has been minimal response from residents to our request in mid-July for each to indicate whether they are interested in receiving community information via email, versus placing a hard copy in their in-boxes. Therefore . . . .

Thank you for your cooperation.

Jill

Jill Revere,
Director of Services.

A MEMORIAL DAY EVENT

April 15.

TO: All Residents.

FROM: The Manager of Resident Activities.

Many of you cannot attend the upcoming city Memorial Day ceremony, and would yet wish to be reminded of those who gave their lives in the service of our country. A resident has kindly organized a Memorial Day event for us. It will be held in the Century Room. The program involves both local Military and our own Veterans. A copy of the event announcement is included below. Please join us.

Betty Mason

Manager of Resident Activities

A MEMORIAL DAY REMEMBRANCE TO HONOR THOSE WHO SERVED AND GAVE THEIR LIVES

WEDNESDAY, MAY 30th. AT 2 PM IN THE CENTURY ROOM

DETAILS

THE COLOR GUARD OF THE 2ND EXPEDITIONARY FORCE, USMC
WILL PRESENT THE COLORS.
MUSIC BY A BRASS ENSEMBLE FROM MARINE BAND, POINT
PROSPECT.
TAPS BY A MARINE CORPS BUGLER.
THE GUEST SPEAKER IS CAPTAIN HUGH BOSELLI, USN,
COMMANDING OFFICER, USS LONGMEADOW (CCG 21).
THE PLEDGE OF ALLEGIANCE LED BY ROBERT REEVES, AUTHOR
AND WW II VETERAN.
BOB SERVED AS THE EXECUTIVE OFFICER ON A KOREAN WAR
DESTROYER.
REMARKS BY MR. STEPHEN REESE. A WW II VETERAN AND
RETIRED COMMANDER, USN.
STEVE WAS A NAVAL AVIATOR. HE FLEW MANY TIMES OFF
AIRCRAFT CARRIERS.
REMARKS BY SEA CADET JUDY COLLINS, EVANS BATTALION, NAVAL
SEA CADET CORPS.

IF YOU WOULD LIKE TO HAVE LUNCH AT 12:15 PM ON MAY 30TH
WITH ONE OF THE MILITARY, SO INDICATE ON THE SIGN-UP SHEET

Hans Christian Andersen's advice to the elderly,
"Learn to be forgotten and yet to live."

A SHORT RENDEZVOUS ON VETERANS DAY

A nearby hamburger eatery is very popular, particularly with the college crowd. Customers over ninety years of age are infrequent visitors. They get noticed and even get another glance. Their handicapped parking space is occasionally occupied. It has little practical appeal to young customers. They would be ticketed. A car was parked in the handicapped space of that fast food restaurant on Veterans Day.

That day was as good an occasion as any for an elderly man to eat his lunch at this well patronized eatery. He ordered a double patty hamburger, french fries, and a large drink.

The old Veteran picked up his food and seated himself among a crush of college students and other young customers. He began to eat. Partway through his meal another elderly gentleman, carrying a cane and his food tray walked slowly up to the old veteran's table and asked him, "Mind if I join you?"

A conversation ensued.

"I'd be delighted," replied the elderly gentleman.
"Thanks so much," said the man with the cane.
"I'm sure you remember that today is Veterans Day," he added.
"I sure do," was the answer.

They munched on their food for a short while. The man with the cane continued the conversation.

"Did you ever serve in the military?"

"Yes, I did. I served in the Marine Corps during World War Two."
"I served in the Navy during the War." added the man with the cane.
"Then we were both in the same Service."

They looked admiringly at each other and smiled.

"I served with the Marines in the Pacific."
"You did? I was at Pearl Harbor on December 7," said the old man with the cane. I served on battleships."

A small group of college students was eating at an adjacent table. One of them began to overhear the two old men while they conversed. After a while, he nudged a companion and pointed to the two elderly men. Some of the college group began eavesdropping on the conversation.

"I spent 30 years in the Navy."
"I spent two and a half years in the Marine Corps."

The Navy man began reminiscing.

"Would you object if I told you a short story about World War Two?"
"Of course not," replied the Marine, "Go right ahead."
"Well here goes," he added.

"Earlier this morning I was reminiscing about my time in the Navy during the War. I distinctly remember an incident that happened to me on a truly special day. I'll tell you about that day that was at the tail end of the War.
By then I'd served on Navy ships for three years. A couple of buddies and I were drinking coffee on the mess deck. We were crabbing about rough seas during the last few days. Suddenly we heard some loud noises. The ship's horn started making

short blasts. Then we heard the sound of hurried footsteps on the deck. The row got louder. There was lots of hooting and hollering. The whole place got into an uproar. It startled us. We just stared at each other.

Nobody had felt the ship shudder from a direct torpedo strike. It didn't seem like it was going to sink. They hadn't sounded general quarters. We were all curious. The three of us got up and aimed for the quarterdeck. We then heard someone yelling.

"The War's over! The War's over!!!'

Those words sure got our attention. We pushed our way up the ladders and joined in the shouting. I was so excited to hear the news. We decided to let off steam. I slapped everyone I could on the back. Real hard too!

I'm sure you also remember a lot about the War. I knew I'd remember that particular day for a long, long time. We were all so glad to hear the War was finally over.

That was quite an event! You know I never did hook up with my best Navy buddy after I returned to civilian life. I wonder where he's living these days"

The tale was over.

"What a great story!" said the Marine. "Thanks so much."

Their conversation continued. They both agreed that an important part of military service was patriotism and serving the United States.

"Isn't it such a different world now?" said the man with the cane.
"I was only twenty two when I joined the Marines. The world sure has taken a different slant. Times have changed so much."

"That's for sure," replied the retired sailor.

"Yes it is. But when all is said and done today is a very important day for us and our country."

They resolved that this was the day they must always remember their buddies.

The sailor added, "So many of us oldsters have passed on. You don't meet too many World War Two veterans these days, and especially one to reminisce with."

The disabled man finished his meal and rose to leave. Their conversation briefly continued.

"I'm so glad we had this chance to talk," said the man with the cane.

"Yes. It was a pleasure to have your company. Today of all days."

"Thanks for an unexpected conversation, and such a good lunch together.

I'll remember this meeting."

"I will too," was the answer.

"Thank you too. I hope we'll meet again. Why don't we meet here again next year? I'd like to hear about your service in the Marines."

They shook hands and smiled at each other as they left.

The college students were visibly touched as they eavesdropped on the two old Veterans. A serious group discussion ensued ensued about how times have changed. Someone asked the others a question about joining the Navy.

A LOW CALORIE MENU

The following is a dinner menu at a retirement community. The chef's name is Harry. Communities encourage dieting and promote exercise to maintain good health. Seconds are always available. Some residents tend to ignore their cholesterol levels.

SOUPS

CREAM OF ASPARAGUS EN CROUTE
BAKED FRENCH ONION WITH GRUYERE CHEESE

SALADS AND APPETIZERS

HOUSE SALAD WITH DRESSING OF CHOICE
BUFFALO LOIN EN TARTARE
SHRIMP COCKTAIL

ENTREES

ROTISSERIE CHICKEN
SERVED WITH A BAKED POTATO AND STEAMED VEGETABLES

GRILLED T-BONE STEAK
SERVED WITH HOUSE VEGETABLES, ROASTED BUTTERED
SQUASH AND ROASTED POTATOES

FRESH FISH OF THE DAY
SERVED WITH A BAKED POTATO, PEA TENDRILS AND SPINACH

GRILLED SCALLOPS
SERVED WITH STEAK FRIES, HARICOTS VERTS AND RED PEPPER ROUILLE

HERB ENCRUSTED HALIBUT AND FETTUCCINI PASTA
SERVED WITH A PARMESAN CREAM SAUCE, ASPARAGUS TIPS, ROASTED TOMATOES WITH PECORINO CHEESE

CHICKEN BOUILLABAISSE
SERVED WITH A FENNEL SAFFRON TOMATO BROTH, ROASTED GARLIC POTATO PUREE AND CARROTS

DESSERTS

LEMON MOUSSE NAPOLEON WITH BERRIES
CHOCOLATE MOCHA ROULADE CAKE

A PASTRY CHEF'S CREATION OF THE DAY
ICE CREAM AND FROZEN YOGURT. ASK FOR DETAILS.

TRAIN TRAVELS

A combination of captivating grandchildren, time, and infatuation with railroad sleeping cars are a perfect combination. During your old age, you can enjoy traveling the old fashioned way and periodic family visits. Geographically dispersed grandchildren make for more pleasant train trips. You have more time to anticipate the welcoming committee at the final destination.

Train travel is a fine opportunity to observe this country, and to think about it all. There is much to be watched as a long distance train rolls along. New vistas attract your attention and fascinate. Two days and nights on a train provide many opportunities for the train rider to see and reflect on swiftly passing features and occurrences. This includes things such as a striking white cotton field in the Arizona desert, the Washington coastline and San Juan Islands, the Great Divide, a red tail hawk hovering in Oregon, a dove perched on the limb of a live oak in Texas, and weedy old US Route 66 that runs for several miles alongside the railroad track.

There is a sign in West Texas that advertises.

Tombstones for Lease

An advertisement in Louisiana that states.

FRESH BEEF JERKY
Smoked More Than 30 Days

Then there is the sign in Missouri that reads.

NEVER DISPOSE OF YOUR PERSONAL BELONGINGS ALONG THIS ROAD

Landscapes are memorable and distinctive, such as an instant and front view of the Illinois State Capitol in the early morning sun as the train swiftly rolls through the city streets. Or a battered and minuscule rural home in New Mexico with its outdoor privy. Or a couch in the open doorway of a boxcar, occupied by an independent traveling man. In the Chicago suburbs, you can ride alongside what is claimed to be the longest, widest, dual level, colored, and continuous graffiti mural in the world.

Trains get sidetracked, but never a passenger while staring out of the window. There is too much to absorb. Staring out of lounge car windows is a delight, and so are the grandchildren at the other end. On arrival, you immediately have things of interest to tell the grandchildren. You can say you rode the rails in style, thought about many things and saw much more.

LONG DISTANCE TRAINS AND CONTEMPLATION

Riding the rails across the country can be referred to as a thinking man's way of travel. A passenger travels on the conveyor belt of American life. Some options for in transit travelers include counting telephone poles or freight cars, reading a book, dozing, or just plain thinking. Here are some of the wry thoughts that recently entered into a train rider's head.

- Why do people allow themselves to be rushed to a hospital in an ambulance, with a blaring siren knowing they may return home with an acute hospital infection? Take Lysol with you.
- Think about the last time you responded to the questions in a personal medical history questionnaire. If you checked YES in response to questions about your medical conditions, more often than you checked NO, then you are now well beyond the threshold of old age.
- Ask an emergency-room patient why he swallowed that brass button. He casually replies "I didn't do it on purpose."
- Why doesn't a bio-medical designer develop a hospital bed that prevents the patient from always sliding down to the foot of the bed?

- Too many doctors are involved in caring for my health these days. Not one of them has shown any concern about what will eventually produce my death.
- Elderly folks often end a phone conversation by saying "I must hang up now, I need to get to the john."
- Did you know that you will never get to a ripe old age if you keep eating hospital food?
- Why don't we have a medication that makes retirees feel excited or exuberant about entering a hospital?

A PASSING GENERATION, AND A LETTER TO THE FAMILY

May 30th.

Greetings to my family members,

I have a humble reason for writing this letter. You may be curious about what urged me to write. My cousin Fred triggered this urge, and the fact that he's no longer with us. I'm now also aware of a unique family situation.

You've all heard that Fred died last week. I must say how sad I grieve the loss of this relative. These feelings triggered some thoughts that I now need to share. There is not a good or bad reason to write letters. I've never written to so many of my relatives at one time. My rare correspondence with any of you occurred around birthdays or Christmas. That's the extent of it.

After hearing that cousin Fred died I realized I'm the family's last living relative of my generation. That means I'm your oldest living relative. The family tree remains the same, but only a single, living link remains. Family connections within my generation have virtually ended. Yes, they've passed on, and I'm the only survivor.

Fred and Maud, Henry and Betty, Arthur and Lois, Tom and Jill, Fred and Myrtle, Alice and Alfred, Ben, Ernest and Lilly, George and Simone, are no longer with us. All seventeen of them have died. They were my brothers, sisters, brothers-in-law, sisters-in-law, and cousins. They were dispersed around the world. I'm the remaining one. What qualified me to be the only one left? What caused me to become a family rarity?

At a future date, one of you will communicate to you that my time also arrived. No one will remain in my generation. Family history will continue. An elderly family member of the next generation will assume this exclusive position. One of you will become the last survivor.

I know you'll understand my reason for contacting all of you. My thoughts are often about our family. I wish you all many more years of happy living. That's a part of what earthly existence is all about. We're born to live and to die.

With much love,

David

A very old relative.

THE HISTORY LADY

The History Lady is a native of California. She is a unique person and a versatile historian. This lady is a public lecturer dedicated to enchanting the lives of senior citizens by bringing back memories of earlier days and times.

For the past eighteen years, this wonderful visitor, with a charming sense of humor has visited local retirement communities every month to entertain the elderly. For more than an hour she speaks naturally, spins stories, and maintains a fast-moving, informative and entertaining dialogue with her audiences. She brings several large containers that hold a potpourri of knickknacks and memorabilia to be used as her props. The History Lady excels in historically rooted narratives and continual banters with her large audiences.

Her programs focus on notable and scarcely known individuals and incidents. These topics are linked to the same month as the day of the month when she delivers her witty lectures. The information she shares with her audiences ranges from trivia to significant historical details. She makes rapid-fire references to politicians, poets, inventors, attires, food habits, inventions, explorers, consumer items, social patterns, fads, prejudices, music, novel products, artifacts, and historical figures.

At the end of each presentation, the audience has been entertained, educated, charmed and provoked. Residents are encouraged to ask questions. At a recent "History Lady" session, the attendees learned about Lawrence Welk and his disciplined approach to music, Henry Ford and the wages he paid his employees, Abraham Lincoln and why he grew a beard, what the seven points on the Statue of Liberty stand for, S & H Green Stamps, the origin of Wendy's Restaurants, what Bobby Soxers wore in the '50s, Stephen Foster and his music, the source of the Mississippi River, milking stools, the person who introduced the first bikini to American society, the penny ice-cream cone, contraptions to squeeze orange juice, famous Americans born in July, crinolines, and slop trays. These are a small number of the many topics her audiences attentively listen to her discuss.

The "History Lady" is a veritable institution. She is an exceptional person and the rage of retirement communities throughout the region. What a lovely and generous lady. Her life is dedicated to educating and entertaining senior citizens. She is always welcomed. This experience is retirement community education at its best.

GREENING IS OF IMPORTANCE TO RETIREES

Some retirees promote social and environmental causes. Their promptings include agitating for a cleaner environment. Others simply bellyache about the quality of air in general, and air conditioning settings in particular. It behooves residents to advocate on their own behalf, as well as to do this on behalf of like-minded people. Some feel obligated to encourage their retirement community managements to advocate for them.

The following exchanges occurred during an open forum involving residents and staff.

Q: "When will we start using re-circulated water here, Ms. Clooney? The building next door does."

A: "Thank you for your question, Ms. Jones. It will cost us $550,000 to install the proper connections. We simply don't have the money to hook up to the local re-circulated water line."

Q: "I plan to buy an electric car. What arrangements have you made to charge electric cars in the garage?"

A: "We don't anticipate having any electrical outlets for these cars for another year. We have not allocated funding in the capital budget."

Q: "Why can't we get the fountain out front to work again? It was built to spout water in the air. It never does."

A: "The city has issued a water conservation directive that forbids fountain water squirting up more than six feet high."

Q: "So why not just shoot the water up five feet?"

A: "Because the city has to get a formal operating request form. We'll submit one as soon as we can."

Q: "When will you submit the request?"

A: "We have that on our list of things to do, Mr. Jones."

Q: "Why are so many flowers planted out front? They waste water."

A: "We recirculate all the water in the garden areas, Ms. Joske."

Q: "Do you recirculate the fountain water?"
A: "Yes we do."

Q: "Madam, when can I get my shower head fixed? It leaks all the time. We're wasting water."
A: "Thanks for your question, Mr. Epstein. We'll send a maintenance man to your apartment to fix it immediately. Roberto is a darned good maintenance man. He'll fix your problem very quickly."

A PARODY
THE MAINTENANCE MAN AND A BATHROOM SHOWER

You sometimes know if a person has been imbibing. A recent retirement community experience might have confirmed this.

"If Mr. Epstein talks to me again like that, I'm going to quit," said Roberto, the maintenance man."
"Let's try to understand the situation, Roberto," said Arthur, his supervisor, "Tell me what happened?"
"He told me to stay calm!"
"That's an interesting comment. Were you that agitated? What were you doing at the time?"
"I was standing in the shower stall repairing his shower head."

"What happened?"

"He decided to help me fix the leak. He then got in the shower stall with me. Then he then sat down on the shower seat and laughed at me."

"Roberto, you know you must never involve residents in repair work."

"I know that. I think he wanted to show me how smart he is."

"How smart do you think he is?"

"I don't know."

"What did he do then?"

"He reached over and turned on the cold water."

"So you both got wet?"

"Yes, we did."

"What happened then?"

"He yelled at me, and I yelled back."

"What did he say in reply?"

"He told me to stay calm," he replied.

"What did he do after that?"

"He got out of the shower and began stumbling around the bathroom."

"Do you think he'd been drinking?"

"Yes, that's likely."

"Did he hurt himself?"

"No, he just got more upset."

"What did he say when you left his apartment?"

"He told me to keep calm!"

"Did you apologize?"

"Yes, I did, and I don't know why.""

"What did he say in reply?"

"He told me to stay calm!"

"He's persistent, isn't he?"

"I'd better keep away from his apartment."

"Do that. In the meantime, I'll talk to Mr. Epstein."

"I want to stay away from showers stalls. Someone else can repair our water leaks."

"That's not a bad idea, Roberto."

"He's a likeable guy usually."

"I know that, Roberto. Why don't you go home and have a couple of drinks? But not in your shower. Just stay calm!"

FIXING RESIDENT MOBILITY AND INSTABILITY

On a recent evening, the community's residents established a new parking record for motor scooters parked in their dining room parking area. More than the usual number of scooters showed up. They were parked there while their owners ate dinner. Management may have to provide drive-by food service if many more residents start driving scooters.

That evening, six motor scooters were parked as their owners ate. A close examination of these scooters showed various distinctive designs and features. This included a mottled navy blue and emerald green design, a vivid pink one, high and short horn tones and large white-wall tires. There was a large three-wheeler, and a rare model that can only run slowly. Scooters are marvelous contraptions that can turn on a dime.

Dining-room servers very promptly removed scooters from the dining room after their owners were seated at table. They parked them in the designated parking area. There are no designated handicapped parking spaces in the dining room parking area.

After scrutinizing all these parked scooters, one can observe a number of walkers, used by less severely disabled residents. That evening seven walkers were parked there. They were lined up in a single row in the main parking lot. The lot is often full on Friday evenings. A few residents are pleased to have their walkers around at the conclusion of the Friday happy hour.

The styles and décor of walkers have also changed. Improvements to hand brakes are a significant modification. Newer models have brighter coloring. High style walkers have larger wheels. Some baskets are large enough to carry medications and an occasional dinner roll.

As the number of mobility devices increases, management may be obliged to hire a valet service to park all the scooters and walkers. There were thirteen of both these types of mobility devices parked in the lot that Friday. This number is very close to capacity. On that day, a record was established for all these conveniences. Management must ultimately consider construction of a new mobility devices parking lot. It must have a single parking level, several handicapped parking spaces and no speed bumps.

A third mobility device needs mentioning. Some residents carry canes. Cane models and their features are too numerous to detail here. Some canes are antiques, just like their owners. Others are in need of repair, just like their owners. Cane owners invariably present dashing personal appearances. Walker owners often get more easily stressed out. Cane owners seriously dislike being weaned from a cane to a walker. Individuals who carry wooden canes are more distinctive in appearance and have a debonair look. Cane owners are relaxed strollers who do not push a stroller. Canes are stylish and compliment their blasé owners. Walkers can make you look older. Who likes to be seen trundling a walker? If a gentleman carries a cane, his chances of being dated by a cane-carrying lady are vastly greater. This phenomenon was verified by a Friday happy hour cane carrier. She always carries a cane, even though she may not need to.

In the final analysis, scooter owners are racier than walker owners, and cane owners are sportier than scooter owners. Some say cane owners are more sophisticated than walker owners. This may leave the impression that walker owners are at the bottom of the social order. There is no pecking order.

After finishing dinner the handicapped resident smiles and waves to his server. The scooter owner asks him to bring his mobility enhancement contraption to the table. The server skillfully glides the scooter to the owner's table. Departure from the dining room is invariably smooth. On the other hand, a walker is un-dramatically pushed to a table. One server can bring two walkers to tableside simultaneously.

It has been said that scooters make a much grander exit from the dining room than walkers, unless a wheel needs oiling. A decided advantage of carrying canes is their owners are allowed to carry them to the dining-room table. A cane user sometimes twirls his cane while exiting. He might even raise an eyebrow as he passes a scooter owner. This clearly indicates a superior mobility complex.

COLD CASH . . . . EASILY FOUND AND UNRETURNED

The garage was dimly lit, yet it was bright enough for him to observe a rectangular piece of colored paper on the floor beside an adjacent car. A closer inspection indicated that it might be a dollar bill. Once in a great while he found a dollar bill at a Wal-Mart store. He usually kept it. Who cares about a buck? Another buck was right there on the floor, just waiting to be confiscated.

He picked up the piece of paper and got into his car. He soon realized he was staring at a brand new bill of exchange. It was pure United States Treasury paper currency. All one hundred dollars of it. Cash in hand! Cash he could spend!

He quickly glanced around the garage. Nobody was around. He had time to consider his options. Several ideas came to mind.

Break the bill into twenties. Keep $80 and turn the rest in to the front office.

Break the bill into tens. Keep $90 and turn the rest in to the front office.

Drive right out of the garage and quickly spend it on a pair of new pants.

Call the owner of the adjacent car and ask her if she has lost a $100 bill.

Inform her that he found a $20 bill, and wanted to return it to her.

Give the bill to charity.

Turn in the $100 bill to the front desk. Claim it later if no one claims it.

Place the bill back on the floor.

Place the bill in a dark corner of the garage. Keep an eye on it and reclaim it a week later. No one would have found it.

Report to the front desk he had lost a one hundred dollar bill.

A decision was easy. He notified the front desk he had found a new $100 bill. Later that day the adjacent car owner phoned the front desk to say she had dropped some money on the floor near her parked car. The front desk told her the owner of the car parked next to hers had found the money. The receptionist then called him to say his parking neighbor had reported the loss of some cash.

Later in the day he delivered a one hundred dollar bill to her apartment. She thanked him for returning it, and asked "Where's the other $100 bill I dropped?" She firmly added "I definitely dropped two $100 bills on the garage floor near our two cars. I want both of them returned to me now."

He was severely taken aback. Such a mess! He surmised that earlier in the day a shrewd "finders keepers" resident had found both $100 bills and absconded with one of them. He decided he should have told the woman he only found two $20 bills on the floor and was now returning both of them. After all, it would be his word against hers.

CHATTING UP AND DOWN AND IN AND OUT AND NEVER SIDEWAYS

Riding an elevator can be boring, unless you are a passenger riding an elevator in the Empire State Building. Elevators that descend into coal mines are more perilous. Either way, elevators are a convenient form of public transportation. Some riders believe elevators have ears. This is why some residents keep mum on elevators. Other riders cannot believe what they sometimes hear.

These contraptions can be an impersonal mode of travel. They usually provide opportunities for brief verbal exchanges, or they only operate to display public announcements and news bulletins. They are convenient facilities for riders who want to pop their ears on long rides. From time to time elevators break down. This will ruin your day if you work in a coal mine. If you live in a retirement community, a broken elevator provides a new topic to crab about. Coal miners recover from these traumas much faster than retirement community residents.

Elevator rides are not terribly thrilling. They are safer than airplanes, which go up, down, and sideways. Elevators do not usually go sideways. Riders have less intense conversations on packed elevators. An exception occurs when a rider states "I'm sorry" after treading on another resident's toes.

Observing other riders is captivating. Shy residents are less frequently disposed to get on friendly terms with other riders, even during prolonged elevators rides. It sometimes takes three consecutive up and down rides to establish a brief acquaintance. The short vertical travel distances of most elevator shafts necessitate squibby conversations, unless more talkative riders hold the elevator doors open on a floor landing until the elevator lets you know it is peeved.

Elevator conversations can be terse, spicy, dicey, boring, zesty, or snoopy. They are seldom impassionate, stimulating, or exceptionally enervating. Here is a summary of what has been heard during elevator travel between the floors of a retirement community property.

"What floor do you want?"
My grandson loves to push the buttons."

"Please, move to the back of the elevator. There are folks waiting here that have walkers and scooters."
"Hold on to your dog, Ms. Benton. I don't like him sniffing me."
"Whoops, I forgot to push my floor button."
"I thought the employees were supposed to take the freight elevator."
"Young man, I know you pushed all those floor buttons on purpose."
"' I see you've been shopping at Nordstrom's. Did you get any good buys?"
"Did you know Mary Anderson had an accident. She fell down and broke her hip this morning."
"Oh, I thought this elevator was going up. What a nuisance."
"The elevator has now stopped on at least six floors."
"Why not join us for happy hour on Friday? Oh good!"
In a loud and cheerful voice, and very early in the morning
"*GOOD MORNING FOLKS*!
Did everyone sleep well last night?"
"Hello, John! We haven't seen each other in ages. Have you been in the nursing center?"
"Now that Ms. Evans has gotten off the elevator I need to tell you she . . . ."
"Did you hear that the Director of Facilities quit?"
"Isn't the new dining-room furniture ugly?"
"Hello, Nurse! You're making your rounds early today."
"Nancy Jones' new hairdo looks terrible."
"I don't think we should have to put up with that."
"No thanks. You get off first."
"I waited a long time for this elevator. I guess the other one must be broken."
"Did you smell Ms. William's perfume?"
"Here, you dropped something."

"Good afternoon, Mr. and Ms. Jenkins. Are you both settling in well?"
"What's your first name again?"
"That wasn't a nice thing to say about Ms. Robbins, or her dog for that matter."
"Wait, let the passengers exit first."

For some, elevators can become a vital means of communication. Even more important than transportation.

A rumor is circulating that a retirement community is planning a happy hour for its irascible residents. They are to stand in a stationary elevator jammed between two upper floors.

CHARADES AND ELDERLY ENTERTAINMENT

Retirement communities sometimes organize their own entertainment. It requires considerable creativity and inventiveness. Success does happen. On the other hand, the quality of performances may be unpredictable and amateurish. Group efforts often demonstrate that considerable amateur talent is available to carry off an event. The main purpose is to make people laugh or groan, or both

To set the stage, a spirited group of residents decided to organize a charade. Planning began with a group meeting.

CHARADE PLANNING

"What do we want to do?"

"How about someone who steals dinner rolls from the dining room and gets caught?"

"No, that's dumb."

"How about having someone being thrown out of our retirement community?"

"That'll upset management."

"What about a resident getting lost in a gambling casino?"

"We can't do that either. Pricilla Jones lost quite a bit at last week's gambling outing. She might think we're poking fun at her."

"That's right."

"How about one of our residents giving birth to a baby girl?"

A heated discussion followed.

They all finally agreed.

"Then we'll do something about a very old lady who gives birth to triplets."

"OK. Let's move on."

ORGANIZING

The actors created and rehearsed their performance.

They assigned parts, including the selection of a pregnant retiree.

Her husband was not consulted since he only had a very small part.

A large pediatric staff was recruited.

No instruction was given.

They found what they thought would be suitable hospital garments.

They discussed ways to impress the audience.

They arranged furnishings including a makeshift delivery table, overhead lights and a waste basket.
They almost forgot suitable baby bassinets.
The more they prepared the more excited they all became.
They considered their best approaches to organized mayhem.
They eventually decided they were ready to perform.

The community management was notified that a pregnant resident was about to deliver a baby. Amid this surprising announcement, a staff member initiated a quick search for the baby's undisclosed father. No official announcement was made on the impending birth of triplets within the community. The residents did not wish to distress the newly hired Programs Manager.

ON THE DAY OF THE CHARADE

Management organized a pre-concert baby shower to introduce residents to the upcoming event. Anticipation was high. A large turnout was predicted. Someone prepared an event program that included pink paper and ribbons. A baby shower was organized. The residents chuckled when they heard Ms. Bennett would play the lead role. Her tummy suited the role. Besides she had a strong voice which, when cued, would colorfully enhance an occasional groan.

The cast dressed. They prepped carefully, and told the anesthesiologist he was far too prone to hog the stage.
Expectations were high. Mr. Allen disinfected the auditorium (delivery room) by spraying the air with water from a spray gun. He deliberately sprayed some resident.
The announcer called for silence. The chattering ceased. The audience became eagerly attentive, and the performance got underway.

THE PERFORMANCE

Things began with very tentative applause.
A nervous member of the cast kept tugging on his face mask.
The serious part of the evening was about to begin.
The cast assembled around a smiling and over-confident Ms. Bennett.
She often winked at her friends until a cast member told her to stop.
Crisp and urgent medical instructions were given.
The surgeon asked Ms. Bennett how she was feeling.
She forgot her lines and replied, "I feel just great."
The crowd laughed at this unrehearsed and poorly timed remark.
The father, appearing wilted, wrung his hands and periodically smiled weakly.
Mrs. Bennett practiced a deepish sigh which made Mr. Mallory catch his breath.
The moment of birth arrived.
With great flourish, the surgeon produced a large baby doll. It was fully dressed and had a broad and toothy grin.
The audience noted the baby wore long plaid pants.
Some ladies smiled.
Several men appeared bored.
The surgical contortions continued.
Another baby was delivered. It was a second and larger baby doll. The surgeon displayed it to the audience and waved it around his head with considerable pride.
The doll wore glasses and red shoes.
There was loud cheering and more laughter.
Someone noticed the second delivery doll also had a smile on its face.
Ms. Smith sighed.

Medical instruments, in the form of kitchen utensils, again flashed dramatically.

The cast revealed exceptional medical skills.

Another baby doll was delivered. The surgeon twirled a brown teddy bear in the air for the audience to see.

He glanced at the bear's face, frowned and quickly shoved it under the delivery table.

Someone had gone too far. They had switched a bear for a doll.

The surgeon looked around for the proper type of newborn.

Another doll was eventually found on the floor in the back of the room. It kept repeating the words "Da! Da!"

Each delivery was observed with "Ooohs" and "Aaahs."

The audience was surprised when a fourth baby doll was promptly delivered from under the table.

It appeared as a total surprise.

The anesthesiologist grinned from ear to ear and pointed at all the dolls, and the bear.

There were comments about how beautiful each baby looked.

The bear was so much appreciated that it was passed around for the audience to see.

Someone in the audience talked about naming the bear.

The exuberant mother was wheeled out of the delivery room with a big smile. She had an open expression of accomplishment.

The baby dolls and teddy bear were returned to Ms. Sullivan's grandchildren.

With wide grins they had seriously observed the machinations involving their props.

The audience clapped and demanded more.

The cast considered an encore.

There were no more dolls or bears. Anyway, four was enough.

They took another bow and energetically congratulated themselves.

There was sustained cheering, and some whistling.

All forgot their aches and pains.

POST-PERFORMANCE EVENTS

The charade was a success.

Ms. Bennett phoned the babies' father and thanked him for his emotional support. She asked how long ago had bears' genes entered his ancestors' genetic makeup.

The community's policy manual was amended to allow the babies to be cared for in the retirement community.

Management organized a baby naming contest.

The residents demanded a sequel.

Life returned to normal.

CHRISTMAS CAROLS

Some social events are long remembered by retirement community residents. The notice in the community's mail room announced that a children's choir would visit the community and sing carols for them. The day of the performance arrived.

They flew right out of the bus. Everyone laughed and gabbed.

A few of the children stared in wonder at all those old folks with their walkers.

Another wanted to go to the toilet.

The auditorium was packed.

The children sang in tune and did so well.

The concert was beautifully performed.

The solo soprano was ethereal.

They sang two encores.

Following the concert the staff served them ice cream and cookies.

The boys chatted with the residents.

The choir promised to return next year.

They would again ask for ice cream.

The entire music program will be long remembered. So would those nice-looking boys with such perfect voices.

MISCELLANEOUS COMMENTS BY RETIREES

Comments and questions heard around a retirement community may not always sound genteelly or be delicately stated.

"Did you drink your prune juice today, Mr. Jones? Here, drink it now."
"Molly's not wearing her wrist alarm band."
"Push the nurse call button harder."
"Maybe you're not getting enough fiber in your diet."
"Using a walker will help."
"How did your visit to the doctor go?"
"But I only gained ten pounds."
"Someone bumped into my car in the garage."
"I ran marathons when I was younger."
"We'll get your groceries up to your apartment as soon as we can."
"Try using a laxative. Regularity is very important."
"No, Ms. Jenkins, there are no bedbugs in your apartment."
"We must take you to the emergency room, Mr. Chung."
"When can I return home from the nursing center?"
"Good morning, Ms. Prentice. It's time to take your medication."
"How do I find a family doctor around here?"
"The shot won't hurt, Ms. Thompson."
"Don't tell me you've lost your door key again."

CCRCs AND THE U.S. MARINE CORPS

This report is written in memory of a military approach to community discipline and good social order. Residents of retirement communities rarely confuse their facility with a United States Marine Corps Recruit Depot. Managers avidly avoid hiring retired USMC drill sergeants. Yet drill sergeant types have been hired. The residents then get to experience the consequences of a regimental approach to retirement living.

The new employee had a strong military bearing. He displayed a solid and traditional military demeanor towards the residents. He truly believed they were his recruits at the Marine Corps Recruit Depot.

The words, thank you, you're welcome, and please, would have been appreciated. The residents might even have felt kindly on seeing the words "Semper Fidelis" tattooed on the back of his hands. This Drill Sergeant type occasionally demonstrated the kind of caring a recruit received on the first day of boot camp.

He voiced his commands loudly and convincingly. Drill Sergeant training had conditioned him that way. He could be heard all the way into the garage. If the community had a brig, a few residents would spend time there. He was taught that good conduct and military discipline are essential features of military leadership. But it was unappreciated at this worksite.

He obviously felt that familiarity breeds contempt.

We wondered how he conducted himself at home.

We questioned how long he would remain on the job.

The Marine Corps promoted him after he had worked for three months in the community.

They transferred him overseas.

He now carries a machine gun and still barks out crisp orders.

His squad appreciates and admires him. They respect his firmness.

His commanding officer has named him for a promotion.

God Bless our ex-employee and the United States Marine Corps.

God Bless America, and the retirement community!

This is an appropriate time to reflect on retirement community staffs. Misfits are extremely rare. Employees are dedicated, commute long distances, are concerned for resident welfare, and grateful for their jobs. They greet you by name. They listen. Their voices have a kind tone. They smile and work long and hard. They sometimes get frustrated. They should all make more money.

THE AUTHORS CLUB AT A RETIREMENT COMMUNITY

M y retirement community is blest with innovative and creative residents. Over the years, some of them organized evening programs that provided opportunities for residents to assert mind over matter. One such group is the Authors Club. It was formed by an animated and dedicated resident. She felt the authors in the community would profit by participating in regular manuscript readings and discussions. The group's goal was to share compositions, read excerpts of their works, and discuss each other's creations.

A recent Club meeting began with the participants listening attentively to the reading of a triple rhyming poem. They next reviewed a scientific article. A lighthearted composition about rabbits and carrots ensued. A book review followed. The subject involved a Frenchman who had witnessed the advance of the German Army into France in 1940. At the close of the evening, a writer named Justin read a composition about a retiree who regularly sat on the balcony of his apartment and curiously observed the passing scene below.

The essence of his creation follows.

JUSTIN'S WORLD AS SEEN FROM HIS BALCONY

J ustin slowly walked onto his balcony. These days he was obliged to take less frequent neighborhood strolls. Occasional short walks were supplanted by sitting in a chair on his balcony. The balcony eventually became his primary means of enjoying the outdoors and neighborhood activities. It produced no exercise. This regimen became his way of inspecting his surroundings.

Justin seated himself in his favorite chair and peered over the balcony railing. He closely examined his surroundings. They had remained much the same since yesterday. Only transient pedestrians and some loud traffic reminded him that the neighborhood scenery did change. Men and women, old and young, passed by. Some strolled, others hustled.

He noticed a little boy walking beside his mother. They held hands. Together they reached a nearby intersection. Firmly clasping her son's hand they began crossing the street. Midway across the boy came to a halt, right in his tracks. He stared transfixed at an oversized yellow truck with a shovel contraption attached to its front end. The truck driver stood tall beside his truck as he deftly manipulated two long yellow levers. They both caused the massive shovel in front of the truck to go up, down, or sideways. The driver clearly demonstrated professional front shovel operator skills.

In an effort to get him moving the little boy's mother impatiently tugged on her son's arm. He strongly resisted, and continued to stare wide-eyed at the yellow truck with its large yellow shovel. He couldn't help noticing that the shovel operator was amazingly adept.

There and then the little boy decided he wanted to operate a yellow truck with a big shovel up front. He would receive lots of pleasure by operating a large shovel. He might eventually operate it more smoothly than the man he now watched so intently. Having arrived at his momentous decision he happily skipped across the street, hand-in-hand with his mother.

Justin, the balcony occupant, now turned his head towards a siren that sounded across the way. An ambulance appeared. It was headed towards the adjacent skilled nursing center. The ambulance parked in front. Two uniformed attendants jumped out and opened the rear doors. At the same time, a car drove up and parked behind the ambulance. A woman emerged. She watched apprehensively as the attendants prepared to transport a patient. Solicitous words passed between her and the attendants. A gurney appeared from the care center. It carried an old man. There were brief greetings between the nursing care staff, the old man, and his wife. The attendants began to load him into the ambulance. The woman held her husband's hand as long as she could. The balcony occupant glanced away. This was a private moment.

Justin looked back towards the little boy and his mother. They had both watched this poignant event. Right then and there the small boy made up his mind that he would never want to be an ambulance driver. Yellow trucks with giant yellow shovels were unquestionably in his future. He decided ambulances would never offer him the same kind of enjoyment, even though they made a great deal of noise.

Justin's gaze shifted to the retirement community driveway. A small white bus was parked there. It was loading some elderly residents for their weekly trip to a local shopping center.

The little boy simultaneously turned his attention to the bus and its boarding passengers. He pointed towards one of the little old ladies who waited in line. She wore a purple hat, a red blouse, and deep red pants. He chuckled at the sight of her multi-colored attire. The color combination struck him as rather strange. He noted that the white bus did not have a shovel attached to its front end.

Twenty years later the boy is a now fully grown man. He happily drives a small white bus. It does not have a large shovel up front. Neither does it have a siren. The man wears a red and purple driver's uniform. Children occasionally stop in their tracks and stare at him.

RESIDENTS SHARE THEIR PERSONAL SORROWS

The following note was prominently displayed on the mail room bulletin board in a retirement community.

FROM THE SMITH FAMILY

Dear fellow residents,

My sincerest appreciation for your sympathy, kind thoughts and wishes!

I just can't thank you enough for the support you have given me during Bill's sickness and at the time of his death.

Your notes, cards and phone calls have sustained our family during these difficult times.

I intend to respond.

My family also wishes to thank you. You have all been so kind and considerate.

Please make donations to the local cancer society.

Thank you all so terribly much!

Molly Smith and Family

"Before you speak, listen. Before you write, think. Before you spend, earn. Before you invest, investigate. Before you criticize, wait. Before you pray, forgive. Before you quit, try. Before you retire, save. Before you die, give."
—William A. Ward

PART II
A POTPOURRI OF RETIREE CONVERSATIONS AND ATTITUDES

AN ALTERNATE APPROACH TO FINDING A RETIREMENT FACILITY

The following discussion involved an elderly couple. With much curiously they recently visited several retirement communities in the vicinity of their home. They were actively researching retirement community facilities.

"What do you think? We've read ten brochures and visited over seven retirement places in our area."

"I'm not sure. I might want to move into The Regency. But they're quite expensive. They have a decent care center though."

"I like The Embers. They have the best food."

"Mabel, we really didn't visit a single place that served good food."

"That's not fair, George. You can't expect home cooking in these kinds of places."

"I expected them to have less chicken on the menu."

"It's what your parents enjoy eating."

"That's their choice."

"We did meet some nice people."

"You don't meet many nasty people in a retirement community."

"I wonder what they thought of us."

"Probably a couple that enjoys gossiping."

"The cost of The Princess is more affordable."

"Yes, we need to be concerned about medical care."

"The Embers just increased their monthly fee."

"Everything's going up."

"How about the size of the apartments?"

"The Regency's not too bad."

"Well, I just don't know."

"You seemed to enjoy the place."

"I just don't know."

"What didn't you like?"

"They all seem so severe, and The Willows looks run down."

"We don't have to move there."

"Why do we want to move away from here?"

"You're right, I just want to stay put in our own home."

"I do too!"

"It looks like we wasted over two months of our time visiting those retirement places."

"It was your idea."

"It's not my fault."

"I just want to ensure that you're well taken care of if I died."

"I appreciate that, John."

"Let's chat about all this tomorrow."

"OK. Why don't we visit The Broadmoor tomorrow afternoon?"
"Not tomorrow, dear. I'm playing golf."

RELOCATING HER MOTHER TO A NEW RETIREMENT APARTMENT

E arlier in the day, the elderly mother walked into her newly purchased retirement community apartment. Her daughter had accompanied her on the drive down from Seattle. Several suitcases were delivered to her new home. They shared the unpacking. It took the entire day to bring some orderliness into her future home. Too much time was spent fumbling around the apartment. Nostalgia filled their thoughts. They chatted as they unpacked.

"How do you like it?" the daughter asked.
"It looks very nice, doesn't it?"
"Look, there's a good view from the living-room window."
"That's right."
"You'll be happy here, Mom."
"I'll get used to it."
"What time is dinner?"
"I don't know."
"You'd better check the booklet."

"Where's the booklet?"
"It's on the coffee table."

Mom glanced at the coffee table. She looked past the booklet and stared towards the kitchen. Her mind was made up. She would do much of her own cooking to keep herself busy.

"You don't know anybody here, do you?" asked the daughter.
"That's what I'm concerned about."
"You'll get to know folks here pretty quickly. You're good at that."
"When will you visit me?"
"Don't worry. I'll come back next week. Do you need anything?"
"No. Not right now."
"Will you phone me?"
"Of course I will."
"Look Mom, you have a place over there for your books."

Books were her joy. She had inspected the community's library on a prior visit. It contained an impressive number of books. She was glad.

"That's right," she replied.
"I suppose we need to get ready to go down stairs for dinner."
"Yes, we do."
"I'll miss you, Mom."
"I'll miss you too."
"This is a really nice place. Don't you agree?"
"Of course it is, but I'll sure miss my old home."
"I know. I know you will."

"I wish you could email me," the daughter added.

"Don't worry, I'll settle in quickly. You watch. They might have some computer classes here!"

THE COMMUNITY FIRE ALARM SOUNDS

Muriel and her husband had recently moved into their apartment. While watching TV the facility's audible fire alarm started blaring over the wall speaker in their living room.

"My, what's that noise, Jim?"
"I think it's the fire alarm, dearest."
"Who set that thing off?"
"I didn't. I think the front office did," Muriel replied.

A loud announcement was made over the in-house loud-speaker in the apartment.

"This is a drill. Please proceed to your designated security area and remain there until we sound the all clear. We will shortly announce further instructions."

"Do you think an apartment's really on fire?" Muriel asked.
"Maybe, who knows?"
"What are we supposed to do now?"
"Try reading the resident manual, dearest."
"Where is it?"

"You had it last, sweetheart."

"No I didn't, you had it. I saw you reading it."

"There's not enough time to find it now," said Jim.

"Call the front desk," Muriel requested.

Jim called.

"It's busy," he said.

"Did you find the resident manual?"

"No. Besides this isn't the right time to look for it."

"We'd better do what the man said and move to a secure location in the building."

"Where's that?" asked Jim.

"I think we have to go to the stairwell, and walk down two floors," said Muriel.

"Why two floors?"

"Beats me!"

"Can we walk to either of the two stairwells on our floor?"

"I don't know," she replied.

"Which one is the closest?"

"Let's see. It's the one to our left," Muriel replied.

"Do we need to take anything with us?" Jim asked.

"No, just put on your shoes."

"I will," he replied.

"I'll take my needlepoint."

"What do we do with the dog?"

"He can lead the way," she replied.

They calmly exited their apartment, very confident this practice had been well organized. She would now get to meet a few of her new neighbors.

AN INNOCUOUS TEA TIME CONVERSATION

Tea-time conversations pass the time away. These chats can be stimulating, energizing, and profound. Others are extremely dull or boring.

"Do you ever go walking?"

"I try to walk every day for about half a mile."

"I never walk. It's too hard on my feet."

"Did you know that one mile equals 2,213 average steps?"

"Where did you learn that?"

"My grandson told me."

"Where do you take your walks these days?"

"I walk around our neighborhood. Usually at seven in the morning."

"I'm not up then. Besides, I always watch TV before breakfast."

"You need to walk more. It will do you good."

"So does sleeping in bed."

"Did you know that the only parts of the human body that keep growing in older people are their noses and ears?"

"Where did you learn that?"

"My grandson told me."

"Do you wear any special shoes for walking?"

"No I don't."

"I often watch people walking from my balcony."

"That must be very exciting. Do you count the walkers?"

"Not anymore. I recognize most of them."

Several eavesdropping residents started to examine their neighbors' noses and ears.

"I get to meet all kinds of people while walking."
"I don't need to leave our lobby to meet all kinds of people."
"Did you know that a person's nails keep growing for some time after they die?"
"Who told you that?"
"My grandson did."
"If you don't get out and walk you won't get to meet any kids and their mothers."
"I don't always like to meet kids. I prefer taking trips on the bus."

Two nearby residents began to examine their nails.

"You need to try walking with me. We won't walk too fast."
"I'll pass on that. Why don't you invite Joe Walters? He might enjoy that."
"Did you know our next local eclipse of the sun will appear in eleven years?'
"No, I didn't. I assume your grandson told you that."
"That's right."
"What did Joe Walters say?"
"I asked him, and he turned me down. I don't know anyone else to contact."
"Why don't you just continue walking on your own? You can always hum to yourself."
"I do."
"What else has your grandson told you?"
"He asked me if my family background includes a relative who has flat feet."
"You can't have flat feet and do that much walking."
"I don't."
"Did he talk to you about energy conservation?"
"No, he didn't."

On they went. Chatting passes the time away, and can produce strange facts.

LEARNING ABOUT RESIDENT AVOCATIONS

Not all teatime chats are boringly dull. Some conversations are revealing. New residents often turn out to have particularly interesting backgrounds. Mabel was chatting with Pricilla Jones; a recent move-in. Pricilla is petite, soft-spoken, and shy. The conversation went like this.

"It's good to have you with us, Pricilla. You must be tired after unpacking."

"Yes, I'm wilting and want to get to bed early."

"Where did you live before you moved here?"

"I'm from Prospect, Arkansas."

"That's nice. What did you do back there?" asked Mabel.

"I worked for the Salvation Army."

"That must have interested you."

"Yes, it did."

"I'm sure you did some other things to keep you busy."

"Oh yes. I did volunteer work at the 'Y.'"

"That also sounds like interesting work."

"Yes it was. I also made occasional out-of-town trips."

"Where did you go?" asked Mabel.

"To Las Vegas."

"That's an exciting city. What brought you there?" she asked.

"The gambling."

"The gambling!?"

"Yes the gambling."

"Tell me about that," Mabel asked. "It all sounds so interesting."

"Well, I flew there regularly to play poker."

"Really! Did you win much money?"

"Oh yes, I've won up to $8,000. Once in a while I lost money."

"Goodness gracious," said Mabel. "How did you go about doing all that?"

"The casino provided me with a plane ticket and a beautiful suite. They also provided my meals and drinks."

"That sounds just like a retirement community."

"I was well taken care of if that's what you mean."

"Did you ever return home broke?"

"Only once. They gave me a first-class plane ticket and drove me to the airport.

They were extremely generous," Pricilla replied.

The subject shifted.

"We organize a poker game here every week. The players gamble for a tenth of a cent a point," said Mabel.

"Oh, you do? Where do they play?"

"In the Rose Room," replied Mabel.

"I wonder if I might participate in the action?"

"Of course you can."

"Did you say a tenth of a point?"

"Yes, one tenth."

"That's not much."

"Really? That sounds like a lot of serious gambling to me!" Mabel exclaimed.

Pricilla thought about that and then added, "Maybe I can get them to jack up the ante."

Mabel said to herself, "I can't wait to tell my friends about her. Things will change around here. I'm sure glad I don't play poker."

The next day Pricilla phoned the Activities Department. She signed up for the resident poker game. Future sessions would certainly be more interesting. She might even try to up the ante. The poker players will find it harder to win now they must play against that sweet poker-faced lady from Arkansas.

Then there are the monthly bus trips for residents to gamble at a local casino. The dealers there will call her "that delightful old lady who arrives in a retirement community bus and wins." If she had a sizeable gambling loss she knows she could ride the retirement community bus back home for free. The driver might suggest she ride up front.

VISITING HARRY

The doorbell in Harry's apartment rang several times.
Harry was sitting on the toilet. He hollered, "Who's there?"
Abe, his friend was standing at the open front door and hollered back,
"It's me, Abe."
Harry replied, "I'll be there in a minute."
"Why don't you just ask me to come in?"
"I can't," said Harry. "I'm sitting on the toilet."
"What's my request got to do with sitting on a toilet?"
Harry replied, "Sitting on the toilet takes a lot out of me, Abe."

"Well stop being so busy, Harry, and ask me in."

Harry finally greeted Abe at the door.

"Hello Abe. How are you? You look great! What can I do for you?"

A pause while Abe mulled things over.

Abe replied impatiently, "Darn it, Harry I've been standing here for ages."

Another pause.

Harry asked, "What do you want to bother me about, Abe?"

Another pause.

Abe replied, "I don't remember."

"Well that's too bad! Why don't you come back when you remember why you dropped by."

Abe left, wondering whether Harry really was his good friend.

ENTHUSIASTIC OCTOGENARIANS GO BOWLING

A group of residents decided to go bowling. They asked the community Activities Coordinator to organize a trip to the Ace Bowling Alley. She felt uneasy and checked with the nurse. The nurse commented, "If they want to cripple themselves that's their fault. They're all grown up." She predicted no one would sign up. Ten did.

The bowlers were excited when they boarded the community bus. They arrived at the bowling alley. Here are some comments made during this hearty and outlandish experience.

"What's your bowling average?"
"I don't know. I've never bowled before."
"We need to rent bowling shoes."
"My shoes fit me perfectly."
"I can't believe what's going on."
"I used to pay twenty five cents a game."
"That was before bowling alleys were invented."
"You really don't know a thing about bowling."
"Don't be so critical."
"Hand me a new ball. I can only get one finger into that big hole."
"Who's keeping score?"
"I don't keep score. It's bad for my nerves."
"You're up. Bowl like you really meant it."
"My ball didn't come back on the return."
"You haven't bowled yet."
"Ouch, I hurt my arm."
"You signed up to go bowling, didn't you?"
"That's seven gutter balls you've bowled."
"Who said this was going to be easy?"
"Try bowling the right way for once."
"Did you see that? His ball just took out the wood divider."
"Do rebounds count?"
"Darn, I fell down again."
"Your ball was clocked at four miles per hour."
"At least it arrived there."
"You just bowled a 36 game."
"Was that your best score ever?"
Someone commented, "So much for championship bowling."

It was time to drive home and start coping with upcoming aches and pains. They returned with broad smiles on their faces.

There are three ways to improve your bowling game: Keep your eyes on the pins, cheat, or watch someone else to see how it's done. All three techniques will work for seniors.

ABBEY DISCOVERED SOMETHING IN THE SWIMMING POOL

Abbey Rutherford invariably went swimming at 8:30 in the morning. She had only missed one swim in the community pool since moving in three years ago. This was her important daily exercise, and an essential daily routine.

As usual she walked into the pool area, very ready for her swim. After removing her bathrobe and glasses she walked to the edge of the pool. Abbey always checked the water temperature by dunking her big toe in the water. She disliked swimming in cold water.

She stood at the edge of the pool. Aghast, Abbey stared hard at the water, and then took a big step backwards. Abbey kept staring. She frowned. Yes, she definitely saw a brown object floating in the pool. It floated towards the pool's edge, as it bobbed up and down. This situation was simply awful and must be reported immediately. How dare a resident do that while swimming in her pool!

It was early. The staff had scarcely arrived to work. She hurried upstairs to report the crime, and arrived at the reception desk.

"Melody, I want to report a very bad situation. There's something brown colored floating in the swimming pool. It ruined my morning swim!"

"I'm so sorry to hear that, Ms. Rutherford. I'll call the maintenance man. He'll check into the situation. "

"Please do that, immediately."

"Thanks for alerting me, Ms. Rutherford. Why don't you go back to your apartment? We'll keep you informed."

"Thanks, I will."

Ms. Rutherford returned to her apartment. She quickly made the first of several quick phone calls to her friends.

"Emily, guess what I just saw in the pool!"

"What?" asked Emily.

In very graphic detail she described what she imagined had happened and added,

"I definitely saw it."

"You must be kidding," replied Emily.

"I'm not!" retorted Abbey.

Emily quickly phoned four of her friends.

Meanwhile, the maintenance man set up the "THE POOL IS NOW CLOSED" sign outside the pool area and then walked to poolside. Yes, something was bobbing up and down in the pool. He scooped it out and examined it. It was a small oval and brown piece of wood. He also noticed a scooter wheel at the bottom of the pool. He fished it out and reminded himself to ask Ms. Rutherford if both these items belonged to her.

A while later.

"Ms. Rutherford," said the receptionist, "We want to report back on that brown thing you saw in the pool."

Ms. Rutherford interrupted her. "I'm glad you handled this situation so quickly. I hope you thoroughly purify the water and reopen the pool as soon as you can. Maybe you need to empty the pool."

The receptionist looked at her, smiled and replied, "Ms. Rutherford, that brown stuff you saw in the pool was just a small piece of wood. We removed it." She decided not to ask Ms. Rutherford if she had lost a scooter tire.

Word about the pool contamination had already spread like wildfire throughout the community. No one questioned her story. Ms. Rutherford was always right.

TRIPLE SCOOPS ARE DE RIGUER

An enticing ice-cream parlor is located near a retirement community. A small group of residents periodically patronized this delicious emporium. These high cholesterol level folks decided to organize another visit to their favorite haunt. They were set for a satisfying and tasty experience. The group assembled in the retirement community lobby.

"It's ice-cream time!" Marion very loudly proclaimed to the group.

Marion is not an eight years old girl. She is over eighty and the prime sponsor of those escapades. The parlor had recently designated Marion their "Senior Ice Cream Lady of the Year."

"Who's ready to go?"
"We all are!"
"Let's go then," said a ninety-one-year-old.

Time was wasting. Off they scrambled. Several pushed their walkers as fast as they could towards the ice-cream parlor. It was a Senior Olympics event, now known as the seniors' ice-cream dash around the corner. They attracted attention. There was the usual jockeying to be the first in line for ordering.

They arrived and were warmly greeted. After all, they were very old customers. Their sustained loyalty qualified them for free ice-cream samples.

"Who has the discount coupons?"
"You do."
"No I don't."
"Who's buying?"
"You are."
"No I'm not."
"Everyone goes Dutch," said Marion.
"Are you sure you have the coupons?"
"They're in my purse."
"I want three scoops, please. One chocolate chip, one coffee, and the other coconut parfait."
The ordering rattled on.
"Give me nutty cocoanut," requested another.
And so on.
"Don't forget to give them the coupons. We get one dollar off each cone."
"That's great!"

Deciding on their flavors was the hard part. It always took a lot of finger pointing. They smiled or nodded when they received their cones. There was little time or inclination to inspect each other's choices. Slurping was de rigueur.

"Shall we eat inside or outside?"

They decided to lick their cones in the parlor, surrounded by several grinning high schools students. The homeward-bound conversation was about their preferred flavors. There is nothing like a senior who ignores an endomorph diet plan.

HOLIDAY DECORATIONS

It is the peaceful seasons of Christmas and Hanukkah at a retirement community. The time is 10:15 am. Ms. Connie Clooney, the Managing Director, is chatting with Mr. Wilberforce, a member of the Holiday Decorations Committee.

Connie says to him, "I need your feedback about this year's holiday decorations. I hope you realize there's a limit on what we're able to spend, and how much we can display for the holidays."
Mr. Wilberforce replies, "Yes, Ms. Clooney, I understand. But you need to know a Christian resident here told me the Jewish folks have more decorations on display than we do."

That's not quite accurate, Mr. Wilberforce," replied the director. "I had our Facilities Manager check on this situation yesterday. She was quite pleased with the displays."

"I don't agree, Ms. Clooney. A couple of us also checked. We found that the Jewish residents have four Menorahs on display this year. We only have two crèche scenes. That's not fair."

"I'll have to check into that again, Mr. Wilberforce."

"Thank you, Ms. Clooney. May I make a comment? We're pleased to read that the Christmas dining-room menu refers to a Christmas Dinner and not a Holiday Dinner. That's so very nice of you."

"Thank you for telling me, I'll pass that on to the chef."

"Thank you, Ms. Clooney."

The time is 11:15 am on the same day.

"Thanks for dropping by, Mr. Moses," says the Managing Director. "What can I do for you?"

"Well Ms. Clooney, a couple of our Jewish residents toured the public areas yesterday. They counted the displays of Christian decorations, such as nativity scenes, poinsettias, and angels and found that they have more of their items on display than we Jewish folks do. Would you please do something about this?"

"Yes, Mr. Moses," replies the director. "I'll have our Director of Facilities look into the situation and report back. I'm sure we agree that the holidays are a time for sharing."

"Yes we do," he replies. "Thank you so much, Ms. Clooney."

The time is now 1:45 pm.

"Hello Connie, this is Betty. You need to know that Mr. Porter in Apartment 12 and Ms. Mashamo in Apartment 21 just dropped by my office. They objected to all those Christian and Jewish decorations around the building. They said they're pointless and want to talk to you right now about removing them. They sounded very serious."

WATER IS SIMPLY EVERYWHERE

It was evening. He returned to his apartment, unlocked the front door and entered his living room. He felt a squish, squish, squish sound underfoot. His ears heard a squish, squish, squish sound. He was actually squish-squishing around in his nice living room. The floor was taking on water. This was a new experience and a liquid surprise. Someone was playing a very bad joke. He must act quickly.

The resident phoned the front desk. They hurriedly sent a maintenance man up to his apartment. He arrived and knocked on the apartment door. The resident yelled, "Come on in!" He entered and stared wide-eyed at the watery floor.

"What happened?" he asked.
"Someone played a joke on me," the resident replied.
"Where's the leak?"
"Who knows."
"Let's find out where it's coming from." said the maintenance man.
They searched the apartment. All the faucets were turned off and there were no leaks.
They agreed the water leak originated somewhere else.

The resident concluded, "If gravity serves me well it comes from the apartment above us. The water must be running down the building's interior walls and into my apartment."
"That makes sense," the maintenance man replied.
They called the front desk.

In the meantime the apartment continued to accumulate water. The resident might need a life preserver.

The receptionist called back.
"We sent someone to check the apartment above you," she said.
"Did they check his faucets and other plumbing?"
"Yes they did. A faucet has been left open. We turned it off" she replied.
"What do you want me to do now?"
"Pack some clothes. We're going to move you to a local hotel while they fix up your apartment."
"Thank you," he replied. Will you pay for my martinis?"
"Check with the hotel manager," she suggested.

He hurried over to the hotel for a martini. The receptionist mentioned their hotel had a swimming pool. He replied he had just come from a swimming pool; and decided not to return to the apartment for his swim shorts.

Three days later he returned to a dry apartment. A repairman had left a life preserver there. The resident who lived in the apartment below his continues to believe he caused all the flooding and damage in her apartment.

A YOUNGSTER CHATS WITH HIS GREAT GRANDMOTHER

A small boy, full of curiosity, chattered away with his great-grandmother who resides in a retirement community. He was full of questions.

"Why do people around here look so old, Grandma Alice?"
"Where do they all come from?"
"Why do they all have white hair?"
"When are you coming home?"
"Ooooo! There's a lady over there with brown hair."
"Why is that old man pushing that thing for?"
"Can I ride on that man's scooter?"
"No, the green one over there."
"Do you like living here?"
"There are lots and lots of old ladies around here."
"Why don't you drive a car anymore?"
"Do you get to eat a lot of ice cream?"
"Look there's a dog over there."
"Is living here fun?"
"Will I ever move here?"
"Is it time to go home?"
"Will you send me candy?"
"Look, Grandma, there's another kid over there."
"I like the swimming pool here, Grandma Alice."
"When will we come back to visit you again?"
"I'll miss you too."

"Goodbye, Grandma."
"Goodbye, Jack."

Alice waved and shuffled upstairs to take a nap.

TEXTING IS FOR THE YOUNG

Helen and her friend Martha were chatting in the computer room. Their conversation went like this.

Helen: "I've attended computer classes here for two years. I still can't figure out all that Internet and computer stuff. On top of that, why does my family expect me to send text messages? I have trouble enough writing letters by hand."

Martha: "I know it's hard, Helen. But you need to keep trying. I work at it from time to time. I don't understand much about all that stuff either."

Helen: "Here's an example of what I'm talking about. I just received a text message from my grandson. I can't understand a thing he said. Here, look at his message. It doesn't make sense. You figure it out."

"hi gm looking forward tyv btw get here at ten cu at my apt and eat befo you lv don't forget to turn the lo it will be gt to cu ttfn bert"

Martha: "Just call him on the phone, dear, or write him a letter. I always phone."

SURNAMES ARE DIFFICULT TO REMEMBER

A resident by the name of Ms. Millie Rappesport, entered the office of Connie Jones, the Executive Director of a retirement community. She greeted Ms. Rappesport, who replied, "Good morning, Connie! May I talk to you about a way to the help the residents remember each other's names?"

"Why of course, Ms. Rappesport," replied the director.

Millie continued, "Like many other residents I'm having trouble remembering the last names of all the residents."

Connie replied, "Yes, Ms. Rappesport, this can be a problem. I wish we could help you."

Ms. Rappesport replied, "But you can."

"I can? How's that, Ms. Rappesport?"

"You need to announce to the staff and residents that they must all change their surnames to **SMITH**."

The Executive Director thought for a few seconds and replied, "Why that's a wonderful idea, Ms. Smith! Yes, it would make life much easier around here."

Ms. Rappesport got up to leave.

"Goodbye, Ms. Smith," said Ms. Rappesport.
"Goodbye, Ms. Smith," said the Executive Director.
Ms. Smith walked out of Connie's office with a very satisfied look on her face.

A GERIATRIC CONVERSATION ABOUT TROWSERS

It is dinner-time and a couple is patiently waiting in their apartment for their dinner companions to show up. Their friends had agreed to drop by on their way down to the dining room.

"You'd better put your pants on, George. The Abramsons will appear pretty soon."
"I still have time," he replied.
"Get them on right now, and pull up your zipper. You forgot to zip up yesterday. Ms. Miller saw you and asked me if you had arthritis in your hands. Besides," she added, "You give the impression you need to wear elastic waist pants."
"That's a good idea."
"Not while I'm around," she said.
"I can always tell my friends that I can't dress myself properly."
"You know how to dress perfectly well."
"I never, ever forget to zip up."

"Yes you do," she replied.

"Well no one can see anything."

"They'd better not."

The conversation topic shifted.

"Are we bringing the wine tonight?" he asked.

"I think it's our turn. Bring a bottle of white wine."

"I think I'll get a bottle of red wine. I prefer red."

"Well, I know she likes white."

"Why don't we ask them what they want?" he asked.

"That will just create another argument."

The doorbell rang.

"They're here!" he exclaimed.

"I told you to zip your zipper."

"I did!"

"Give me a big hug when they come in. Let's give them the impression we're newlyweds."

"Do you really think they'd fall for that?"

"We should always act that way anyway."

"Well, if you insist."

"Check your zipper, George."

He did.

LOST AND FOUND ON A CONCERT TRIP

A group of residents were transported in their community bus to a music concert at a local park. They arrived and found good spots for their folding chairs. Everyone anticipated a fine brass band performance. The concert ended. The residents boarded the bus to return to the retirement community. As protocol required, the bus driver counted the number of passengers on board. One resident was missing.

"We're missing one person!" the driver exclaimed.
"Who's that?"
"Check the list."
"I don't have a list."
"We can't leave here without finding out who's missing."
"Who has the list?"
"I do," said the driver.
"Check the list then."
"I will," said the driver.
The driver checked off names against faces and announced that Ms. Epstein was missing!
"Where did she go?" someone asked.
"Who wants to go and find her?"
"I don't think she came to the concert."
"Yes she did."
"Let's find her before she really gets lost."
"Let's get organized."
"I didn't hear you. What did you say?" asked a resident.
"We need to get organized."
"What did he say?" the resident asked again.
"Talk to the driver."
"What do you think, driver?"
The driver mulled it over and replied, "One of you can walk south and search over there. One of you can walk north and search in that direction. I'll scout straight ahead."
"I hope you know which way is north."
"We need to check the restrooms."

"What if one of you gets lost?"

"We'll watch you."

"How do we do that?"

"Let's get on with it."

"Brilliant," said a resident at the rear of the bus.

"Why don't we call security at the retirement community and let them know about this situation?"

"We can do that later."

"I already have," said the driver.

"Well why don't we drive home and leave it all up to the police?"

"No. We can't do that."

"Listen up ladies and gentlemen," said the driver. "Here's my plan.

Mr. Eddy, you walk south. Ms. Cummings, you head north. Ms. Faber, please check the restroom. I'll search straight ahead."

"I don't have my cane with me and don't want to do a lot of walking," said Mr. Eddy.

"Well you don't have to get involved," said a resident.

"Any other volunteers?" asked the bus driver.

"What did you say?" asked Harry.

"Let's help the driver."

"Here we go again."

"Shush," said a polite lady.

"OK folks. Let's get going with the search party.

Mr. Jacobs, you take Mr. Eddy's place and search to the south," said the driver.

The designated searchers got up from their seats.

Someone suddenly spoke up loudly.

"Well take a look at who's standing at the bus door!" he exclaimed.

"That's Ms. Epstein, isn't it?"

The residents looked towards the open door.

There stood a smiling Ms. Epstein.

Mildred Epstein climbed on board.

There was much clapping and words of relief.

"Where did you folks go? Is this the right bus? Wasn't it a great concert?" Ms. Epstein asked.

"It's good to see you, Ms. Epstein. We were about to call the police."

"We're glad you arrived back here safe and sound, Mildred."

"Thank goodness for our smart driver."

The driver smiled and started the bus engine.

Everyone cheered.

Someone exclaimed that the Mildred experience was better entertainment than the band concert.

A CHEERLESS DINING ROOM CONVERSATION

Two residents are in conversation during dinner.

"Have you visited the skilled nursing center lately?"

"No I haven't. What's going on there these days?"

"You haven't heard about Rachael Jones?"

"No, I've been out of touch with her lately. What happened?"

"She had another stroke. She's flat on her back and can't move her legs. All those difficulties and now she's almost blind."

"That's terrible! How old is she?"

"I think she'll be 93 next birthday."

"Rachel has lived a long life. I guess old age eventually catches up.

I don't want to end up that way."

"Growing old isn't for sissies my dear."

A SOLEMN PAUSE.

"Yes, you're right!"

"I wonder how Jill Stewart's cancer has progressed?"

"I haven't heard."

"Who else do you know who's in the skilled nursing center?"

"Well there's Walter and Maggie."

The conversation continued in this manner during dinner.

ONE YELLOW ROSE IN A SILVER VASE

When a resident dies, management compassionately informs the residents that someone has passed away. Traditionally, a single yellow rose, in a silver vase, is placed on a table at the entrance to the dining room. A memoriam card is added.

Two residents passed by this table and paused to read a newly placed card. Their conversation follows.

"What a shame. He was such a nice gentleman."
"Yes, we'll miss him a lot. Jim was a great golfer."
"I heard you went out with him a couple of times."
"Yes, he was very friendly. A real nice man."
"I just had an idea. Why don't we go to the City Council and request they pass a new Ordinance requiring all local florists to immediately stop selling yellow roses to retirement communities.
It might stop all our residents from dying."
"Why that's a wonderful idea, Betty. Let's do it."
They both smiled.

CLEARING OUT HIS APARTMENT

Their widowed father died in a retirement community a few days earlier. This retirement community's rules & regulations manual read, "Family members or designated persons must remove all residents' personal effects from a deceased resident's apartment within three weeks of that person's death or relocation."

Panic set in. This is a conversation between the father's son and daughter while they sorted out his possessions.

"Where do we begin, Earl?"
"This is just too much. I had no idea he had so many odds and ends."
"We need to get leads on who might buy his furniture?"
"That's a good idea. But I'd like to look it over again before we sell it."
"I thought we'd already agreed on what we wanted to sell?"
"I thought so too. It looks so nostalgic and collectable."
"Look at this photo, Earl. He looks so charming doesn't he?"
"Now's not the time to study photos, Sheila."
"I know that. I want to remember him."
"Well you can do that after you return home."
"What do we do about his kitchen stuff? I don't want it."
"I don't either."
"Let's give it to the Salvation Army."
"I don't have his computer password. Do you?"
"I left it at the office."
"Oh great!"
"What about all his toiletry items? Where can we send them?"
"Down the trash chute, I guess."
"Let's call the front office. They have lists of furniture dealers."
"That's a good idea."
"We need to get a dozen more boxes."
"No, at least fifteen more."
"I sure would like to have his TV."
"Why don't you contact the moving company about it?"
"There such a lot of stuff to dispose of."
"What a lot of memories."

"Do you remember when . . . ?"

"Come on Earl, get to work. We can talk some more at dinner tonight."

"I'll fix us some lunch. No sense in wasting his frozen food."

"What about disconnecting his phone and Internet services? Can we do that later today?"

"No, let's wait until we get closer to finishing."

"How long do you think it'll take to get all this done?"

"Longer than I thought, and with a heavy heart," he replied.

"Before undergoing a surgical operation, arrange your temporal affairs. You may live."
—*Ambrose Bierce*

PART III
RETIREE HEALTH AND WELLNESS

A PUBLIC MESSAGE FROM A SKILLED NURSING FACILITY OCCUPANT

A skilled nursing center patient taped a large handwritten notice outside his door expecting that all who walked by would read it. The message faced the main corridor of the facility. It read.

IF THE DIRECTOR OF THIS CENTER
ENTERS MY ROOM AGAIN TO TALK TO ME
I'LL CALL SECURITY!
I DON'T EVER WANT HIM TO ENTER MY ROOM!
KEEP OUT!
I MEAN IT - KEEP OUT!

This patient must have reasoned that management was unresponsive to his needs. On the other hand, some patients simply prefer total privacy. They may feel compelled to express themselves forcefully, and in plain English.

MAKING SPONTANEOUS HEALTHCARE DECISIONS IN A PARKING LOT

A resident fell and hurt himself in the lobby of his retirement community. This misfortune started a debate among several bystanders who observed the incident. By good chance the harmed person was accompanied by a close friend.

A sensible question to be considered at that moment was "After an individual has taken a fall do you help him get up right away?" A debate on this subject ensued.

"Watch out, Gene, you almost tripped."

"I'm OK," replied Gene. "I can perfectly well see where I'm going."

He promptly fell on his side.

"Holy cow! That was a nasty fall. Did you hurt yourself?" Hugh asked his friend, "Stay on the ground until we get the resident nurse here."

A bystander alerted the nurse.

"I don't hurt too much," Gene replied.

"Where do you hurt?" Hugh asked.

"It's around my hip area."

"Which side?"

"The left side."

Several residents assembled to observe this event.

One of them said, "Can you get up?"

"Please don't ask him to get up," said Hugh.

"He may hurt himself again," said another bystander.

"He looks fine to me," someone said in a loud voice.

"Poor guy, he's flat on his back and everyone's staring at him."

Another one commented, "It looks to me like he can get up."

"Why don't you help him to get up?" asked another observer.

"I'm his friend. Right now he'll do what I ask him to do," Hugh replied.

"Ask him if he can move his leg," someone asked.

"Yes, I can move both my legs," replied Gene.

"There you are. He's not that bad."

"Stay on the ground," Hugh ordered.

"I will," replied Gene.

"What does the law say about all this?" someone asked.

"Probably to quit encouraging him to get up," Hugh directed.

"He looks OK to me,"

"Make him comfortable," another commented.

"Are you comfortable?" Hugh asked.

"Yes, I'm fine,"

The nurse arrived.

"What happened?" she asked.

They told her in great detail.

She examined Gene and said, "I'm glad none of you tried to move him. I believe your friend has a broken hip,"

A bystander said, "We've been watching him very carefully and told him not to stand up."

"That's right," added another.

The bystanders nodded in vigorous agreement.

"That's good, said the nurse.

The observers began drifting away.

Gene and Hugh waited in the lobby for an ambulance.

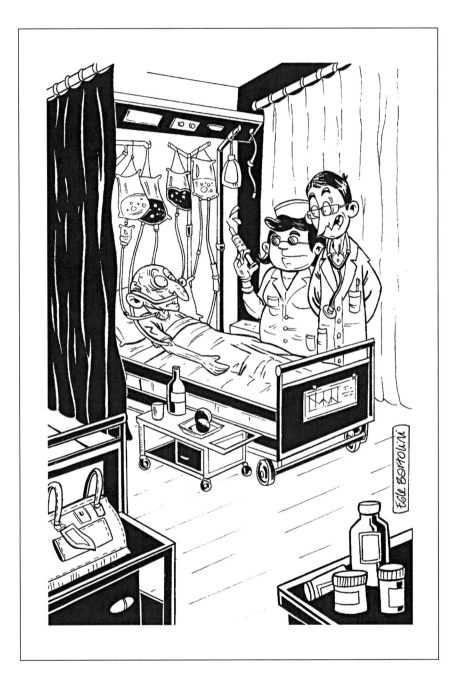

"I have good news for you today Mr. Sullivan.
You should have been discharged two weeks ago."

CONTRASTS IN CAREGIVER INSTRUCTIONS

Information is transmitted by retirement facility staffs to many residents in different formats. A writer's style can vary according to the intent of the message. The contrasting messages below have serious intents and contrasting styles.

THE HOUSEKEEPING DEPARTMENT

CLARIFICATION REGARDING BATH TOWELS AND BED LINEN

A reminder that two sets of bath towels per bathroom are provided. Residents who desire additional towels may request them and they will be provided at a cost of $10.00 per set, as noted in Appendix 2 of the Handbook. If you use Community-provided linens each week the housekeepers will remove and replace your used bath towels. *They will replace the same number of towels they remove for laundering.* For example, if both sets of towels were removed, two sets of towels will be left. If only one set of towels was used, only one set will be provided. Also, each week one set of bed linen per bed is provided (1 fitted sheet, 1 flat sheet, and 2 pillow cases). To request additional towels, contact the front desk.

THE WELLNESS CENTER

WHAT TO DO IF YOU FALL

Stay calm. Do not panic.

Assess the situation. Do you have pain? What part of the body is affected? Can you move?

Know your physical limitations, e.g., past hip fracture, left- or right-side weakness.

Press your lifeline pendant button to activate the first responders to go to your location.

First responders will assess the situation and assist in determining whether you are able to get up independently.

If it is safe for you to get up the staff will coach you on how to get up independently.

If you are unable to get up independently, emergency services will take over your care.

IT CAN BE HELPFUL TO CLEARLY DOCUMENT YOUR MEDICAL DATA

How might individuals simplify the sharing of personal medical information? Here is an example of a practical medical form that can be easily prepared. It contains personal data and enables others to get a quick reading on your medical/personal information and conditions. Someone can help you by typing it. This document may be folded to fit into a wallet.

PERSONAL MEDICAL DATA

MY NAME IS: JOSEPH J. REDSTONE.
DATE OF BIRTH: 6/4/1930. **HOME ADDRESS:**
1234 FRIENDSHIP LANE, TAUNTON, TN 12345.
PHONE/FAX: 222-456-7891.
EMAIL: terry1@myemail.net.
MY PRESCRIPTIONS:
PREDNISONE: 2.5 mg, 1/day. WARFARIN: 5 mg, 1/day
OVASTATIN: 20 mg, 1/day. MULTIQ: 400 mg, 2/day.
BETROX: 0.4 mg, 1/day. OSTERPROM: 20 mg 1/day.
SUPPLEMENTS: FERROUS SULPHATE: 65 mg, 1/day.
CITRASTAT: (630 mg), 1/day. B-12: 500 mg, 1/day.
Vitamin D3: 2000 IU, 1/day.
ALLERGIES: DARAZAN and PRETZAR.
MY MEDICAL CONDITIONS & STATUS: I HAVE
HAD PMR FIVE TIMES. NOW IN REMISSION.
I HAVE PERIODIC ATRIAL FIBRILATION. IT
IS UNDER MEDICINAL CONTROL. I HAVE
CHRONIC KIDNEY DISEASE - STAGE 111. I HAD
UPPER AND LOWER SPINE SURGERY TO
CORRECT STENOSIS. I DO NOT DRINK OR SMOKE.
MY HEIGHT: 5' 11". **MY WEIGHT:** 180 LBS.
MY BLOOD TYPE: AB.
MY PREVIOUS SURGERIES: TONSILECTOMY.
DEVIATED SEPTUM. REMOVAL OF NASAL
AND COLON POLYPS. HEART ABLATION.
PROSTATE ABLATION. SPINAL STENOSIS
AND SURGERIES.

MY PHARMACY: ABD PHARMACY, Rita Blvd., Taunton, TE. Phone: 222-444-5555.
MY DOCTORS: Internist: Dr. BROWN, 222-3456, Cardiologist: Dr. EVERETT, 222-333-444. Rheumatologist: Dr. RASHID, 222-666-7777. Anticoagulant Station, Dr. MARMAN, 222-888-9999. Neurologist: Dr. SILVERSTEIN, 222-333-8888.
PERSONAL CONTACTS: # 1. MILLIE REDMAN (Spouse), 222-777-4444. # 2. KIMBERLY SHORT (Daughter), 333-666-7777.
DATED: June 14.

A doctor commented "I'm so impressed with your detailed medical information chart. It makes me want to read it. I'm going to prepare a similar record for my mother." His nurse added "I need to make a copy for myself."

Some good advice for finding a suitable doctor. You can always spot an excellent doctor by examining the magazines he provides for his patients in his reception room. If the magazines are clean and up-to-date he is a brilliant medical practitioner. This is absolutely right. I have chosen all my doctors that way. You are the very best Dr. Lori, regardless of the condition of your magazines.

COMMUNITY HEALTH CARE SERVICES

Peeking at health care facilities in a United States city is quite revealing. A large local CCRC contains four separate units: skilled care, memory support, assisted living, and active living facilities. They have a round-the-clock nurse center. This is impressive. Checking further you discover additional local medical services and facilities. Here are some.

There are four large hospitals within a four mile radius of this retirement community. Also, four clinics, a major cancer center, and two cardiac centers. An eye-care center is nearby. There are several imaging centers in the area. Patient and staff parking are plentiful. Two other retirement communities are located less than a mile away. Virtually all continuing care retirement communities in town provide some sort of shuttle service to and from nearby medical facilities. Over a hundred and forty local doctors are available for patients to choose from. There are no local mortuaries nearby.

This is a very impressive healthcare lineup. It manifests well for the "Great American Dream of Better Healthcare for All." This review might be expanded further by researching and detailing specific medical services offered, and the quality of caregiving.

This plethora of health services compares much more favorably against the medical services offered in a pleasant rural community in Montana. This community has about twenty retired residents, no local retirement facility, no hospital, and one overworked general care practitioner located in a neighboring town. But then they have clean air and quiet rural living.

AN INVITATION TO VISIT A SKILLED NURSING FACILITY

Continuing care retirement community residents are periodically invited to tour their adjacent skilled nursing facility. This gives them an opportunity to preview an important health care service offered by the facility they reside in. After all, they hear a lot about the place. Each tour is well publicized. Here is a community announcement.

LA CASA REAL RETIREMENT

VISIT THE SKILLED NURSING CENTER!

YOU ARE INVITED TO TOUR OUR NURSING FACILITY. THIS IS YOUR CHANCE TO FIND OUT WHAT WE CAN OFFER RESIDENTS WHO MAY EVENTUALLY NEED SKILLED NURSING CARE. THE TOUR WILL BE ESCORTED BY THE NURSING STAFF. THEY WILL ANSWER YOUR QUESTIONS.

TUESDAY, NOVEMBER 14TH AT 10 AM

MEET IN THE NURSING CENTER LIVING ROOM

LOSING A CONNECTION WITH THE FAMILY DOCTOR

Medical care legislation and regulations are sometimes puzzling. Medicare, as well as state health and safety regulations, are no exception. Healthcare facilities must comply with medical edicts. Some care standards may not make sense. Here is an example.

Shortly after entering a nursing care facility a patient is presented with a list of available physicians who are willing to care for him while he is a patient in that facility. The patient then identifies the physician he prefers for his care. If his physician's name is not on this available list he may request his physician's name be added. This physician is then contacted and asked if he would like to have his name included in the list of available physicians (while his patient resides in the nursing center). If he agrees this physician may provide care for his patient.

It is not uncommon for physicians to be unwilling to have their names added to this list of available physicians. The patient is then obliged to select another physician from the list. This patient may be unhappy about receiving care from an unknown physician whose name happens to be on the availability list.

There are a number of reasons for a physician's refusal to treat patients in nursing care centers. For example any or all the nursing care patients in a facility may request care from any physician whose name is on the eligible physician list. Physicians invariably avoid having their names added to a 24/7 consultation list.

Patients typically accept the care of an available nursing center physician. This is an individual patient decision. Such physician rules can be a source of unhappiness for a patient's family and friends. The idea of a strange physician showing up at a sick patient's bedside may not please them.

The reference in this narrative to visitation restrictions and other provisions does not imply a need to question the competency of physicians assigned to nursing care centers. They are invariably proficient. Many skilled nursing patients would simply prefer to consult with their own physician. They are valued. Patients would typically prefer continuity in physician care after being transferred from a hospital to a skilled nursing facility.

MEDICAL ANGST AND THE ELDERLY

Medical treatments are a common conversation topic among retirees. They may be concerned about chronic ailments, pains, X-rays, MRIs, doctors, treatments, recovery, and an occasional headache. Here is a conversation about personal health.

"What did the doctor say?"
"He confirmed that I have atrial fibrillation."
"Refresh my memory. What does that mean?"
"It's the uneven heartbeats I'm having."
"What causes them?"
"Don't ask me. He explained that I have atrial fibrillation. I don't remember all the details."
"How do you know you have it?"

"Well, my heart occasionally beats faster and irregularly."
"All the time?"
"No, just occasionally."
"Now I remember. You've complained a time or two about this, haven't you?"
"Yes, but it won't kill me."
"That's what you said before."
"Dr. Gregory is an outstanding doctor."
"What else did he say?"
"That's about it. He told me my greatest risk is having a stroke."
"That's not good."
"I have to take a medication called heparin."
"I've heard of it."
"Quite a few old folks take it."
"Yes, and they fall down and bleed to death."
"That's a risk."
"So that's another pill you must take."
"He suggested I keep exercising."
"What else did he tell you?"
"I have to take heparin every day."
"Is there a treatment for your atrial fibrillation?"
"I think there is, and it's called heart ablation."
"Does your condition ever hurt?"
"No."
"When do you see the doctor again?"
"In two months."
"Did you take your medication this evening?"
"Yes, I did."

WHICH MEDICATIONS HAVE THE WORST SIDE EFFECTS?

A conversation between two residents on an important top-ic for seniors.

"Why did the doctor adjust your medication? I thought it worked
perfectly well for you?"
"Well it did, and I began to get headaches."
"Didn't you tell me you get headaches with the Flosamix medication you're taking?"
"No, it makes me fuzzy-headed."
"How many medications are you taking now?"
"Well I take Vitrol for my ulcer, Limpor for my bone density, Jaritol for my arthritis, Kopelate for my indigestion, and I sometimes take Reval for sleep. Oh! I forgot I take Walmer for leg cramps. Oh yes, I use a nasal spray. I can't remember its name. That's a lot, isn't it?"
"Well how about the supplement stuff?"
"I'm off all that for the time being."
"What does all that stuff do to your system?"
"I hope it fixes me up."
"Let's hope it avoids your liver and kidneys."
"It keeps the pharmacists busy."
"You help pay their salaries. They appreciate you."
"We used to get free drug samples."
"That was then. But thank goodness for Medicare."
"What gets me is the cost of all this stuff. I do have Advantage

Plan insurance, but it still drains my pocketbook."
"Are you still taking medication for your back pain?"
"No I'm not. The doctor took me off it. It never worked."
"Do many of your drugs make you feel better?"
"Yes, most do."
"Have you taken your pills today?"
"Not yet. I have to get going. I want to pick up a new pre-scription at the pharmacy."

"Just think George, we now have more than
a three years supply of antibiotics."

PHYSICAL EXERCISE CLASSES

Fitness classes are often a way of life for those who value exercise. The following exhortations came from a class leader during a seniors physical exercise session.

"Where's Mr. Jenkins? Here he comes."
"Good morning, Mr. Jenkins. No, you're not late."
"Let's start off by lying down on your backs."
"Keep peddling your legs."
"Did you say that hurts, Mr. Ready?"
"On your feet, everyone."
"Take a rest."
"Reach up! Reach up!"
"Don't feel badly if you can't do it."
"You'll like the next exercise."
"Are you sure you can get up on your own, Ms. Jenkins?"
"No, Mr. Jenkins, we're not here long enough to take a lunch break."
"You look tired, Mr. Robinson. Do you feel OK?"
"You're all doing so well."
"Now bring your hands together like this."
"Faster, Mr. Gallini."
"Arms extended."
"I'm glad to hear this is your favorite exercise, Ms. Smith."
"Please turn more gracefully."
"Exhale slowly."
"Sit down if you want to."

"You're doing very well, Ms. Saperstein. You must have been practicing."
"No, we're not finished yet."
"Does anyone want a drink of water?"
"Let's all take a short break."
"We need to stop chatting and get back to work."
"My, you really can bend over, Mr. Brewster."
"Slowly please."
"Breathe in deeply."
"Here's a new assignment for you folks. We can do it next time."
"This is one you'll all appreciate."
"Only three more minutes, Mr. Jenkins."
"That's enough for today. Now go back to your apartments and take a rest."
"Mr. Jenkins, please don't forget that we start earlier tomorrow."
"You've all been so good!"
"Don't forget to practice."
"See you all tomorrow."

EXPERT MEDICAL ADVICE

Elderly patient become stoic about their health. They are usually prepared for doctors' pronouncements. Here are two contrasting conversations involving different doctors.

A PATIENT'S CONVERSATION WITH HER DOCTOR

"We've examined your MRI, Ms. Wellstone. I have good news for you. There are no signs of a serious problem in your lumbar area. Right now you have no physical changes to be worried about. There's very slight compression in your lower back. It's nothing to be concerned about right now. You don't need to quit playing golf. You could benefit from the exercise. Take Tynelol if you have any mild soreness. The family will be glad to hear you're still in pretty good shape. The important thing is to think about playing golf again."

"Thank you so much. Doctor. I was worried I couldn't play any more golf."

"Come back and see me in six months. We need to keep an eye on your osteoporosis. I don't want you falling and breaking any bones."

She told the doctor she would make another appointment on her way out and added, "I can't wait to tell my golf partners."

"Enjoy your golf!" he replied.

ANOTHER CONVERSATION AT A DOCTOR'S OFFICE

"Doctor, won't you just let me drive my car on weekends, and only in daytime?"
"I'm sorry, Ms. Epperson. The tests indicate you must immediately stop driving your car. Your driver's license must be revoked"
"That's too hard on me, Doctor. How about just letting me drive to the store and back? I need my transportation."

"It's not a matter of restricting your driving. Ms. Epperson. it's about not driving at all."

"None at all? I need my car to get me to the supermarket."

"I realize that, but the law is clear. I'm required to disclose your condition."

"When will this be effective, Doctor?"

"Today, Ms. Epperson."

"Well, I'll have to give the car to my granddaughter."

"That would be a nice thing for you to do."

"Thank you, Doctor."

"Managing elderly caregiving is a tall order in anyone's books."
—Anonymous

PART IV
MANAGING RETIREMENT COMMUNITIES

IT HAPPENS TO BE COMPANY POLICY

Several dictates govern resident life in a retirement community. Here are five of them.

- The Old Testament
- The New Testament
- No particular testament
- The Koran
- The resident manual

You can always appeal the laws of the land, and receive forgiveness for spiritual misconduct. The successful appeal of resident manual rulings can be quite difficult. Most of the twenty eight pages of a typical handbook are dogma. The remaining pages contain commandments. In reality, a handbook lists residency rules and regulations. You must have rules and guidance in close functioning societies.

The preamble to one such handbook states that new residents are welcomed to the community. It urges them to keep their handbooks handy. Copies are known to have been kept by residents' on their night tables beside their Gideon Bibles. While falling asleep a retired attorney occasionally fanaticized about the ways he could undermine his facility's rules. It was difficult for him to stay awake.

Here are a few interesting rules gathered from several handbooks.

- Seventy-two hours advance notice is required to arrange transportation for medical services.

  Does this include pre-planned emergencies, or must an emergency be prearranged?

- There is a $450 non-refundable fee for pets, and all animals must be free of fleas.

  The handbook does not indicate that residents must be free of fleas, ticks and lice.

- The handbook instructs residents they are forbidden to solicit for any cause within the establishment, charitable or otherwise.

  Some residents are charitable cases. They are forbidden to solicit on their own behalf.

- Residents are reminded to give 48 hours' notice if they wish to have three or more guest cars parked at one time by the valets.

  There is no mention of a busload of relatives arriving for dinner.

- Wearing jeans in the dining room is forbidden.

  This rule denied dining-room admission to a woman who wore a pair of $350 designer jeans to dinner.

- On special occasions residents are limited to hosting no more than 16 guests per meal.

Is feeding the poor discouraged. No mention is made about feeding the homeless, or the limit on crying babies that can be invited to the dining room at one time.

- Three weeks advances notice is required if you wish to host a large private event.

  You may have fallen out with one of your guests prior to the scheduled dinner.

- Then there is the facility's compliance with the Office of Civil Rights' Health Insurance

  Portability and Accountability Act of 1996 (HIPPA). This legislation inhibits a resident from tracking a valued friend who has been moved to the skilled nursing center. Blame the government for that one.

In all fairness, retirement facilities must have very clear rules. Particularly one occupied by three hundred determined retirees.

GRINDING TO A HALT

The upkeep of apartment appliances and other equipment in a CCRC is an important task for a Maintenance Department. Retirees may become careless about using or protecting their kitchen appliances. In an ongoing effort to extend the life of apartment appliances the following request was announced to the residents of a CCRC.

GRACEFUL RETIREMENT LIVING AT SAN SOFIA

MEMORANDUM

THE CARE AND PROTECTION OF YOUR KITCHEN DISPOSALS: BULLETIN # 2

February 14th.

TO: All residents

FROM: The Maintenance Department

In Bulletin # 1, about the protection of your kitchen disposal, we listed a number of food items that residents should never put down their disposals. This comprehensive list included bones, pasta, rice, fats and very greasy foods, peelings, bread, toast, pizza crusts, croissants, bagels, English muffins, Danish, donuts and others. In view of continuing and frequent kitchen disposal breakdowns, and the high number of maintenance staff calls to repair disposals we are obliged to request you comply with the following instructions.

ONLY COLD TAP WATER MAY BE PROCESSED THROUGH YOUR KITCHEN DISPOSAL. NO SOLID FOODS PLEASE.

THANK YOU!

Jerry Brown

The Maintenance Department Staff

*"I can assure you, Mr. Jones, your cat will be
extremely well cared for in this establishment."*

SCOOTERS AND RESIDENT SAFETY

The enforcement of resident rules is a thankless task. Here is a memo sent to residents about their scooters.

WILLOW RUN RETIREMENT COMMUNITY

Subject: <u>DRIVING YOUR SCOOTERS</u>

Dear Resident,

The number of residents driving motor scooters has increased significantly. Corridors are more crowded than ever. Some residents complain that scooter owners are driving unsafely. In addition, the Maintenance Department recently reported a scooter wheel was found at the bottom of our swimming pool.

Management wishes to remind residents of the facility's rules for driving scooters. We are again listing them below.

1. Pets are not allowed to sit on drivers' laps. Only in the front basket.
2. Residents are limited to two scooters per apartment.
3. Snow tires may only be used during wintertime.

4. Never pick up hitchhikers.
5. No drinking or cell phoning while you are driving.
6. No decals over 8" in diameter may be attached to a scooter.
7. Viagra advertisements are forbidden.
8. You may not drive your scooter around the dining room.
9. Weaving is a violation.
10. Call the front desk on your cell phone if you lose your way when riding your electric scooter on a shopping trip. We have free pickups within a 5 mile radius of our facility.
11. The Maintenance Department will provide scooter driving lessons. They will also check front wheel alignment and electrical connections. On Mondays they provide paint and dent knockout work to repair bumps and scratches. There will be a nominal charge.

Additional speeding violations will oblige us to install more speed bumps in the main corridors.

If you own the scooter wheel found in the swimming pool, please pick it up at the front desk.

Thank you for your cooperation. Happy driving!

Roger Alderswig

Roger Alderswig,
Director of Administration

ADVERTISING TO SWAY RETIREMENT DREAMS

The retirement community business is competitive. It must be effectively marketed. Communities exist because aging is a very certain and obvious human event. This is another way of saying people live longer. This phenomenon presents many marketing opportunities.

Automobile manufacturers and retirement community managements have very little in common. However, both are adept at merchandizing their products. Their differing promotional strategies help respective consumers recognize their unique brands. The new car smell inside an automobile helps sell the car, whereas retirement facilities never publicize smells. They tout their cuisine, or sometimes their food.

The following are edited examples of the persuasiveness of some marketing brochures.

"The good life awaits you! Indulge your senses in a vibrant and luxurious retirement community. You will find a rich life complete with cultural, social, and recreational activities! You can unwind, recharge, and live the life you deserve!"

"Non-Retirement Living: An extraordinary community where people thrive! An opportunity for every resident's appetite. Dining here isn't what you would expect from a retirement community!"

"We will help you find a quality Retirement Community! By answering a few questions we will match you with the

finest community in your area. Whether you are looking for assisted living, independent living or skilled care, our network of experts is striving to help you!"

"Retirement Living as anticipated! Find comfort and privacy in your own one or two-bedroom residence, complete with a full kitchen, balcony, and individual air conditioning controls. You will never have day-to-day hassles! Thanks to the weekly housekeeping service you can step out and enjoy yourself. Don't feel like cooking? Enjoy sumptuous meals in the restaurant which is open all day!"

"Added to our superb setting in the mountains are all the requisites for gracious retirement living! We have a dedicated staff and offer many services and amenities that will provide gracious living. In addition, because we operate as a continuing care retirement community, residents receive long-term care benefits to help defray the cost of care. Residents will enjoy our fine care center at virtually no increase in their monthly fee!"

Appeals to prospective customers to enjoy an unsurpassed good life need not be interpreted as a hard sell, or as a vicarious approach. It is a serious effort to provide believable comfort and shelter to a customer seeking a nice place to live in. Alternatively it might simply be viewed as listing grilled Chilean Sea Bass on the dining room menu as "Dead warm white fish."

A SKILLED CARE CENTER CONVERSATION

Language skills and job confidence at the workplace can interfere with efficient two-way communications and shared understanding. Misunderstandings can trigger dilemmas in a skilled nursing facility, or anywhere else for that matter. An employee may not clearly grasp the meaning of a question or an instruction.

A nurse's aide entered a patient's room.
The patient greeted her, "Good morning, I've not seen you around before. Are you a new member of the staff?"
"Yes."
"How long have you worked here?"
She smiled and again replied, "Yes."
"The patient again asked, "How long have you worked here?"
"Two weeks," she replied.
"What is your name?" the patient asked.
"Potabo."
"What's your first name?"
"Rosalinda."
"Do you live close to here?"
"I will," she replied.
"Do you live around here?"
"Yes," she replied.
"Do you have a long commute?"
"Every morning and afternoon."
The patient asked her, "Where did you go to school?"
"Boxer High School," she said.

"Have you worked in the caregiving business before?"
"Yes."
"Do you have a family?"
"Yes."
"Will you work on the day shift?"
"Yes, sometimes."
"Have you taken English language lessons?"
"Si."
"Where?"
"At my school," she replied.
"Are you still taking English language lessons?"
"No."
The conversation went no further.
Rosalinda smiled broadly as she went about her work.

Time can overcome shyness and language difficulties. Conversations do get snarled. In the final analysis, very little can replace family caring and support. Practice and patience are required for language proficiency.

A FRUSTRATING EXCHANGE ABOUT BILLING MEDICAL SUPPLIES

This conversation speaks to good communications. It may imply a lack of employee training. It may be due to employee turnover. Frustrations occur when an employee replies, "I can't talk to you right now. I'm going on my break in 5 minutes."

The patient's spouse dropped by the nurses' station.

"I'd like to ask you some questions about my husband's prescription medication bill for last month. We seem to have a billing problem."

"What do you want to know?" asked the LVN.

"Why did you charge me $16 for Mirquest on the 19th, and again charged me $14 for Mirquest on the 21st?"

"I didn't charge you," the LVN replied.

"I know you didn't," said the spouse, "Then who on the nursing staff charged me? Please find out."

"I don't know," said the LVN.

"Why not?"

"It's not my job."

"Then who can I talk to?"

"You need to talk to Accounting," replied the LVN.

"I talk to Accounting about medication billing errors all the time.

When I talk to them I'm told it's the fault of the nursing staff. So when I talk to you, you blame it on the Accounting Department."

"You'll have to speak to management," said the LVN.

"I'm sure you're aware that this kind of merry-go-round goes on all the time."

"I know it does," she replied.

"Why doesn't a member of the nursing staff try to fix things?"

"I'll talk to my boss," she said.

"When will you get back to me on this?"

"Maybe tomorrow."

"What do you mean 'maybe'?" asked the spouse.

The LVN had a busy look on her face.

SEVENTEENTH FLOOR LANDING DECORATIONS

This is all about Lisa, a longtime resident who resides on the 11th. floor of a retirement community. For many years she regularly decorates the buffet table on her floor landing. Lisa is adept at displaying serious and droll figures which she sets out on the table. Push a button on an item and it sings, or says funny things. Figures, fresh flowers, miniature animals, and other articles complement these ever-changing displays. They vary according to the seasons, or reflect a special event.

For example, around Memorial Day a uniformed Marine Corporal and an Army staff sergeant stand smartly at attention on top of the table. If you press the Marine's left foot the Marine Hymn is played (surely by the President's Own). Other red, white, and blue items are also exhibited. Lisa always recognizes 11th. floor residents' birthdays.

Her panoramas are unique and tastefully designed. They convey good cheer and generate resident interest. Residents respond to her sensitive talent and dedication to entertaining. They are continually entertained by a parade of ever-changing displays of topical interest.

Lisa recently placed the following short notice on the landing table. It was cheeky and reflected another focus for her displays. But not a trend. She continually surprises us.

PUBLIC NOTICE

Due to recent budget cuts, the rising cost of electricity, gas, and oil, plus the current state of the economy, the light at the end of the tunnel will be turned off next Monday morning at 9 am.

These displays make us glad we live on her floor.

FLOOR LANDING DECORATIONS (Continued)

A study in Conflict Resolution

Residents occasionally assume leadership roles in their retirement facilities. They become involved in formal interaction between residents and community management. Some residents agree to become advocates, or representative, of their fellow residents. They help organize community affairs, or deals with sticky social issues. This is salutary and appreciated volunteer work.

Differences between residents and management can occasionally test community harmony and resiliency. A person observing such disparities might conclude that the dialogue between the two is akin to a union negotiating with employers.

The following retirement community setting involved residents and management, as they worked to resolve a disagreement. Their differences centered on the decorations displayed by residents in the community's public areas. It included the placement of decorations by any resident on floor landing furniture.

BACKGROUND INFORMATION

The community went to battle stations. No one saw this one coming. The wrangle got as good as it gets. It demonstrated that retirement living can be as exciting as any battlefield.

A person living in his own home can detach himself from aggravations and get some privacy. He might seal his doors, turns off his TV, closes the drapes, and avoids eating out. He does not have to eat in a communal dining room, or share recreational facilities. He remains inside until the all clear has sounded. Tranquility is more difficult to achieve in a retirement community.

Battle lines were formed. Gettysburg would be reenacted. The source of the problem involved a few residents who complained that the decorations displayed in the facility were inconsistent with community decorating standards. These residents reported their anxieties to management. They requested management arrange for the removal of all displayed decorations. Management acted. The accused were not initially informed of this action.

Management later contacted the offending resident decorators and requested they pick up their displays at the administrative office. They were told management had the sole right to place decorations in public areas. There was a feeling displays might cause a poor impression in the minds of prospective residents. Management added that visitors might react negatively to any tasteless displays on the property.

A number of residents were disturbed by this arbitrary action. Most residents remained on good speaking terms. A harsher smile or two was noted. Petitions were circulated. Letters were distributed and phone calls made. No one contacted the police.

DURING A RESIDENT MEETING

Local management backtracked. They announced that in future, before making any significant announcements, they would first consult with the residents. These good intentions were echoed by residents' comments, including "the residents will decide," and "good for management."

The Resident Committee then swung into action. They scheduled a resident meeting with management. Thirty-nine residents attended.

In the meantime, local management alerted headquarters about the communications dilemma. Corporate legal counsel responded that public area displays by the residents were not permitted, and that this decision fully complied with the resident handbook. In addition, such resident displays might trigger issues over property insurance coverage.

Many attendees spoke up during the meeting. Some were applauded. The aggrieved floor landing decorators were warmly recognized for their decorating skills and fine artistry. Residents also commented on:

- "Traditions do matter. The handbook does not trump all."
- "Headquarters may speak to the rules, but this retirement community is a home to each resident."
- "Do not let the minority rule."
- "The handbook is insensitive."
- "Do not make our place a cold institution."

Cool heads were in evidence. Strike action was thankfully averted.

Neither residents nor management would yield. The significant comment, "Someone won't be happy" was whispered around.

What next? Would the handbook remain the law? How would management handle a situation perceived by some as directly impacting creative spirits and resident individuality? Would there eventually be winners and losers?

MAKING EVERYONE HAPPY

The residents were now being openly consulted. Nobody from headquarters management was present at the resident meeting. Someone interpreted this as "Don't fire until you see the whites of their eyes." A compromise was in the offing. People listened to each other.

The handbook is an important community tool. The residents anticipated local management would further discuss the issues with their lawyers. This would indicate an effort to get them to alter their stance. Regardless of the eventual management decision the community made a substantial communications leap forward. Muscular approaches by either side were deemed inappropriate.

Six months later 11th floor decorations were as visible and entertaining as ever. They were a delight for those who studied them. The community was at peace. A renewed worry for the residents was the prolonged time it took to serve food at dinner-time. This clearly showed that tranquility reigned again.

Readers will now have more insight into friendly clashes in retirement communities. Most community dilemmas can be categorized as entertainment at its best. Communities will always be known as places where old folks never die. They simply argue.

A CONFIDENTIAL STUDY OF COMMUNITY ATTITUDES AND OPERATIONS

A SURVEY PROCESS AND RESIDENT QUESTIONNAIRE

Learning more about community residents' attitudes is important to the managers of many retirement communities. Several techniques have been used to accomplish this. One is through attitude surveys. A questionnaire is usually employed to obtain participant feedback. This is a key feature of the survey process. It is designed to better assess residents' feelings about such things as retirement living, the environment, and ways to improve services.

This survey instrument is most commonly used at larger CCRCs to fine tune facility communications and planning. Smaller sized communities may have more intimate and direct relationships with their residents. They may have a lesser need for a formal approach to improve communications, or for action planning. Interpersonal relations, effective strategies and responsiveness are keys to operating success, regardless of community size.

Here are some areas of resident concern that a management group might wish to analyze through surveying.

- Health and caring issues.
- Listening skills and responsiveness.
- Bureaucracy issues.
- Services.
- Facility policies.
- Employee and facility issues.
- Food and service.
- Increases in the monthly dues.
- Scheduled resident activities.
- The residency contract.

It is quite possible that management, prior to any surveying, is already sensitive to residents' feelings in some of these areas

Overall satisfaction levels in a facility are often quite high. The staff is often complimented. Some departments do get poorer grades. A high response rate is typical.

Following is a sample survey questionnaire used to obtain resident attitudes and suggestions.

<u>THE QUESTIONNAIRE INSTRUCTIONS</u>

List no more than five areas of personal concern about community operations or services. We ask you to give brief examples of each item. This will allow management to get a better fix on your specific concerns. For confidentiality reasons some of you may feel uneasy about participating in this study. Therefore, the questionnaire need not be signed. That is your choice.

Thank you for helping us to gain a better understanding about our operations and how we might serve you better. Place the completed questionnaire in the enclosed confidentiality envelope and drop it off in the questionnaire response box in the lobby.

USING THE QUESTIONNAIRE FORM, LIST UP TO FIVE OF YOUR MAJOR PERSONAL CONCERNS ABOUT OUR OPERATIONS AND SERVICES. THEY SHOULD BE AREAS THAT CONCERN YOU, OR YOU FEEL NEED TO BE CHANGED. INCLUDE BRIEF DETAILS DESCRIBING EACH CONCERN. YOU MAY WISH TO TELL US WHAT WE DO WELL. AN EXAMPLE FOLLOWS.

MY CONCERN, INCLUDING SOME ADDED EXAMPLE(S):

It is difficult for us to get satisfying answers to my questions when I phone the staff. Many staff members do not readily answer their phones.

THE QUESTIONNAIRE RESPONSE FORM

MY CONCERN # 1. GIVE EXAMPLES:

MY CONCERN # 2. GIVE EXAMPLES:

MY CONCERN # 3. GIVE EXAMPLES:

MY CONCERN # 4. GIVE EXAMPLES:

MY CONCERN # 5. GIVE EXAMPLES:

COMMENTS;

Signature (OPTIONAL) _____ Date _____

Fold your completed questionnaire and put it in the questionnaire response box. You do not have to sign this form.

THANK YOU FOR YOUR ASSISTANCE!

The Survey Team

A RESIDENT SURVEY FEEDBACK MEETING THAT WENT AWRY

A retirement community conducted a resident attitude survey. To accomplish this, a written questionnaire was circulated. It was completed by most residents. The residents' responses to the questionnaire were then analyzed and a summary prepared for management action. This was done through resident involvement.

Selected residents were invited to attend one of a small number of questionnaire data analysis sessions. The small group sessions were scheduled. Discussions were led by group leaders. The intent of these meetings was to review the prepared summary of the community responses to the questionnaire, and identify the small groups' five most important areas of concern.

This process would move the program towards developing a very short list of the most important areas of resident concern. Management would address these concerns. They would have a clearer understanding of grass roots attitudes and suggested changes, and be in a position to respond as best as it could.

The group leader handed out a two-page summary of the questionnaire. It contained a summation of all the many resident responses. He asked the group to read it. The meeting proceeded.

The Group Leader:
"We now need to identify the five most important areas you believe management might address. Who wants to make a comment?"

Resident 1:
"I do. I think the information you gave us only covers the concerns other residents expressed. It did not address my personal feelings."

Resident 2:
"That's not correct, Mabel. You were part of the survey. You had an opportunity to give us your opinions."

Resident 3:
"I agree with Mabel. All the responses are not mentioned in this summary. The most important thing managers need to do is increase the number of servers in the dining room. You don't mention that in your summary. Besides, we don't need a survey to find out about that."

Group Leader:
"Who else would like to comment?"

Resident 4:
"Residents always complain. Why do they complain so much? How do you think management will react to all this criticism? It's not fair on them."

Group Leader:
"These are not criticisms, Mr. Swift. They're opinions that the residents have confidentially given to us through the questionnaire."

Resident 5:
"Who will present our information to management?"

Group Leader:
"I will."

Resident 3:
"That's not right. You don't know very much about what's going on here. I don't like you presenting the information. Mabel should make the presentation."

Resident 4:
"I want to examine all the written comments the residents made in the survey. I can't work with the summary information you've provided us. Mabel may be right."

Resident 2:
"That's right. How can we trust this information?"

Group Leader:
"The reason we're here is to discuss the written summary I handed out, and then prioritize it."

Resident 2:
"I didn't see anything in the summary about our personal security. Besides they don't sweep the garage floor often enough."

Resident 1:
"We need more transportation to take us to doctors' offices. There was no mention of that in the summary."

Resident 4:
"Your analysis of the survey information will lead us to the key issues and concerns. Let's give this program the benefit of the doubt."

Resident 3:
"I still think Mabel should present the report."

Resident 1:
"I can't do that. I'd be too nervous."

Resident 3:
"Let the group leader do it. That's what he's here for."

Group Leader:
"Let's try again. Who wants to give me their list of most impor-tant items? We can start that way."

Resident 4:
"Yes, let's try again. But first I have a question."

Resident 2:
"I'm sorry to interrupt you. I need to make another comment . . . . "

Something was amiss. Maybe the residents had not clearly grasped what the project was all about. The spirit was there, yet something was missing. The next survey meeting will produce better problem solving success.

TRANQUILITY PROPERTIES, Inc.

A SUPERIOR RETREAT FOR THE ELDERLY

INTER-DEPARTMENT CORRESPONDENCE

MAY 13.

TO: EILEEN McALESTER, CHIEF LEGAL COUNSEL

FROM: RUTH RUSSELL, MANAGING DIRECTOR

SUBJECT: <u>THE FEMALE GHOST OBSERVED IN APARTMENT 378</u>

Eileen,

In response to a request from corporate, I am forwarding additional information on our *resident ghost* experience. We were recently informed by the occupants of apartment 378 that they have occasionally sighted an elderly female ghost in their living room.

It should be noted that this apparition is sufficiently elderly to be accepted by management as a resident of this community. The presence of a middle age ghost would have immediately triggered community age-related admission issues.

Following is an update on this unusual poltergeist experience.

- Both apartment occupants reported the ghost always pushes a walker.
- The ghost is sometimes observed doing moderate physical exercises in their living room.
- Other residents are aware of the existence of this ghost.
- Several residents have urged we set up a motion

detector and camera in apartment 378. The Maintenance Department is looking into this suggestion.

- The Residents' Committee requested we arrange to relocate this ghost to another retirement community.
- The question of general public awareness, and its impact on future apartment sales were discussed with Marketing. They stressed the need for a rigid corporate denial of this situation.
- We have considered moving the existing apartment occupants into another apartment. This is risky, since the new occupants may be more averse to ghosts, however friendly. Additionally, this idea might be seen as recognition on our part that a ghost really exists. Or that this ghost may prefer the current occupants, and then decides to relocate with them.
- An elderly resident suggested we have the apartment detoxified. This suggestion was not heeded.
- We discouraged another resident from setting up his own apartment surveillance equipment to determine the ghost's habits.
- Several residents have requested the security staff maintain a vigil in the apartment. Apprehending old ladies with walkers is simply not in keeping with our policies.
- The facility nurse suggested we contact the Department of Health and Human Services for their regulatory guidance.
- Several residents have initiated a ghost naming contest. The name Beulah was strongly favored from the start. Management did not participate in this activity.
- The residents of apartment 378 have requested a 25% decrease in their monthly dues. We may counter with a lump sum offer of $750, contingent upon the rapid cessation of ghost sightings in their apartment.
- We are not at all surprised at the lively discussion and speculation prompted by this gentle apparition.

- The press has become aware of this situation. They have asked if the ghost had any living relatives in our community. Or if she is a prior resident here. They have requested photographs.

AN UPDATE: I have just been informed that Beulah has relocated to the nursing care center. She was observed in their living room, with a heavily bandaged left knee. Beulah was seated in a wheelchair, eating lunch from a meal tray. This mischievous spirit is especially mindful of the need for a good appetite and her well-being. We will keep you informed.

Best regards.

Ruth Russell

Ruth Russell

THE APARTMENT DUES WILL INEVITABLY INCREASE

Several events attract the attention of residents each year. They include Community Council Voting Day, the 4th of July, and Valentine's Day. Residents never forget to attend the annual meeting when management announces their annual fee increase. Discussions rarely focus on whether there will actually be an increase. This is wishful thinking. The speculation dwells on how much the increase will be. Betting usually begins at 3%. Here is a letter from management on this subject.

RETIREMENT COMMUNITY LIVING, INC.
LAS VEGAS, NV.

June 29

TO: All residents

FROM: Max Smith, Executive Director

SUBJECT: RESIDENT FEE INCREASES

Dear Resident:

Effective April 1, we will initiate a resident monthly fee increase of 4%. The increase for the skilled nursing facility will be 5%, also effective April 1. This action is simply unavoidable given prevailing cost of living increases. Food costs increased last year by an average of 8%. Local wages increased 4%. Property taxes increased 9%. These are examples of increases that compel us to increase your monthly fee.

We have examined ways to reduce retirement community costs, and minimize the dues increase. Several actions will be initiated by management. For example, we wish to announce that the number of dining room dinner entrees will be reduced to three. This will allow us to better manage food costs. We regret this move. Rest assured that the quality of our cuisine will remain at the same high level you are accustomed to. We know you will understand.

Everything will be done to contain and manage our costs. We are committed to providing the highest level of service and care.

If you have any questions please stop by my office, or call Jim Prospect, Accounting Manager (543-8745).

Max Smith

Max Smith, Executive Director

A RESPONSE TO THE MONTHLY DUES INCREASE

M r. Robert Reeves, a community resident, sent the following reply to the Executive Director's letter.

ROBERT JAMES REEVES
APARTMENT 47

November 29th.

Dear Max,

I received your letter about the monthly dues increase, and it bothers me. I have lived here for 14 years. Every year you publish a fee increase. It is usually 3%. Now you announce a larger increase. The Federal government does not always increase my monthly Social Security payments. My pensions never increase. I know you care, and you must make a decent profit. I trust you.

I appreciate the challenges you face in controlling costs. However, you leave me in an increasingly difficult position. At the rate you are going I may be unable to pay my monthly dues, and at the same time maintain a decent standard of living. In other words, if I live to be 99 I'll become insolvent. This is bad news. I may be forced to move in with my son, but then I'll probably have outlived him.

I hope you understand my position.

Sincerely,

Jim

James Reeves

In good and bad economic times retirement community opera-tors are compelled to follow industry and economic influences on price increases. They do not live in a vacuum. The days of the 6% or higher increase may occur again. This may not bode well for some retirees on fixed incomes.

A TESTIMONIAL TO RETIREMENT COMMUNITY EMPLOYEES

This narration is dedicated to the employees of retirement communities. They clean our apartments, work at the front desk, check our temperatures, cook our food, and many other things. They do such good work.

They give you a full day's work.
They never get overexcited.
They know what's going on and don't gossip.
They keep your apartment clean.
They remind you about things you need to do.
They contact you about mail.
They smile at the drop of a hat.
They remind you to pick up your dry cleaning.
They occasionally miss a dusty spot or two.
Many have worked here longer than the residents.
Some would love to retire. But not to a retirement community.
They occasionally cajole you in accented English.
They will clean your oven even though you never use it.
A few commute to work as much as three hours a day.
They are efficient.

It is sometimes difficult to explain things to them.
They are dedicated.
They are dependable.
Some have large families to support.
They respect your privacy.
They chuckle about you behind your back.
You can tease them.
They make your life easier.
They are courteous.

A NICE NOTE FROM THE MANAGING DIRECTOR

The following letter was received by a retirement community resident in response to a request he had previously submitted to management. Managers make every effort to communicate promptly.

RETIREMENT LIFESTYLES, INC.

AN EXCEPTIONAL RETIREMENT FACILITY

Roger McGinley, Executive Director

1235 HEAVENLY LANE
P.O. BOX 8851
PEORIA, IL 22044
Phone: 832-875-9943
roger@retirementstyles.com

May 1.

To: Mr. Patrick O'Hara, Apartment #2430

Dear Mr. O'Hara,

Thank you for your April 28 letter of inquiry. Since you were unable to attend last week's resident communications meeting I am pleased to send you a written reply to your questions.

1. Electric cars.
   We will install charging outlets later this year.

2. Garage parking.
   I plan to complete the study of residents' handicapped parking by the end of next month. We will forward you the results.

3. Security at the S1 Entry.
   Safety and security remain an ongoing priority and I do appreciate your suggestions about exterior door security. We will review this with the Maintenance Manager. He will take action within 30 days.

4. Entryway lighting.
   We have explored costs associated with installing two additional lights near the street. This situation will be addressed next week

We always encourage good communications, whether in group feedback meetings or individually. Thank you for taking the time to share your concerns.

Sincerely,

Roger McGinley

Roger McGinley, Executive Director

CONCILLIATION MAY AVOID THE FINAL STRAW

Anyone reaching a certain age and physical or mental state will inevitably be confronted by a series of lifestyle decisions involving the remaining years of their lives. Assurances of, and confidence in a tranquil retirement are welcome parts of the retirement decisions process. Relocations to retirement communities are usually made with the knowledge that living there will have its ups and downs.

The following presents a snapshot of people relationships in a retirement community. This narrative is not intended to disturb a retiree's faith in relaxed retirement community living. It might persuade a prospective resident to relocate to a monastery.

Some retirees feel vulnerable after handing over a pile of money to a retirement community owner for a pleasant apartment with a view To agree to do this for an uncertain period of residency can increase anxiety. One day an individual is happily living in her retirement apartment. The next day the resident feels threatened because there are rumors of a CCRC default. Age can exacerbate anxiety. Baby boomers have different perspectives and opinions about retirement than previous generation. Why do you trust and whom do you trust?

Retirement community relations are never completely harmonious. This applies to every kind of retirement community. Friendly as well as no-nonsense differences can crop up between management and residents. The extent of these differences varies from community to community. Disputes include the rights of residents to remain in their apartments after becoming debilitated, and being forced to relocate to

Assisted Living. Another area of past dispute concerns the disclosure of community trust-fund information.

A retirement community recently entered a short period of mutual misunderstanding. The following excerpt is from a report sent by a resident to management. It is an example of peacekeeping, and the need for clear steps to resolve differences.

> " . . . . It is surely time to ameliorate a possibly fractious interpersonal state of affairs. We must recognize that our problems will not simply go away . . . . Hence I recommend that steps be taken to initiate appropriate strategies. This proposal outlines the steps needed for change. I submit this strategy to help maintain a continuing and productive relationship."

The following is excerpted from management's response.

> " . . . . we share your desire to continue to improve the working relationships between the residents and the management of the community . . . . As you say, it is in everyone's best interests to have a financially sound community with satisfied residents . . . . It is helpful for residents at large to understand how their voices can best be heard and represented by their representatives."

Both statements indicate serious efforts to resolve differences. Good relationships are the result of "win-win" situations. This surely equals "strong empathy and compassion" in retirement community circles. Communication channels can always be improved.

A WORD TO RETIREMENT COMMUNITY MANAGERS

A conscientious and hardworking CCRC Director may read this narrative as he prepares an important corporate proposal. His immediate task might require the preparation of a strategic plan for the property owners. It may require him to prepare an action plan to better shape future operations. It may require him to increase profits and mesh that action into improved levels of resident care. He applies his skills and knowledge and produces the strategy.

In good faith, and in support of management proficiency, I am persuaded to offer professionals like him my serious advice.

This narrative concerns an executive's ability to effectively and profitably manage an organization. Managerial proficiency is about results. Less effective managers are known to concentrate on mundane operational tasks, such as completing forms or turning off the lights. Their work must more importantly concentrate on managerial tasks, such as creative problem solving, or the development and management of employees. Few managers are so unequal to the task that they "keep polishing brass while the ship sinks."

Positive attitudes, motivation, good business planning, and sound marketing skills are synonymous with management competency. An issue is how to better utilize such management tools to improve performance. This includes areas like preparing an effective mission statement, planning for results, crisis management planning, pay for performance, training plans, and the transparency of residents' rights. Some organizations consider people involvement and productivity improvement to be worthy programs for consideration. The successful use of any of these tools can benefit the culture and operating results of an organization. However, launching any of these programs must be based on an organization's needs. Such tools may get mixed support, both intentional and unintentional. Managers must avoid installing a comprehensive program if the organization does not need it, or will not support it.

Smaller organizations may feel a particular initiative is too academic or speculative, or inappropriate for their specific needs. An initiative might be viewed with uncertainty, or is unnecessary to achieve operating results. Management's vision may be quite tactical. Their priority is to solve immediate problems. This may be wise.

First-line supervisors must realistically focus more on tactical work. This means rapidly extinguishing operational fires. It makes a lot of sense to put out fires in any senior healthcare facility. Yes, fire prevention does require planning.

Management and supervisory turnover is an industry dilemma. Some executives lack adequate training. Some lack experience or the sound knowledge to needed solving people problems. Their management practices are too intuitive. Things seemed to have worked well in a previous job and yet do not do so well now. The learning curve is too steep. Managers burn out. A healthcare professional may have excellent technical healthcare skills and does not easily master the skill of managing people. While observing these managerial challenges a resident may feel he is working among the gladiators in the Roman Coliseum.

Business acumen is important. Intuition can have a place when based on professional experience. The bottom line is affected if residents are not reasonably satisfied, or if the social climate in a community fails to adequately attract new residents. A genuine goal is to generate an environment where the residents feel they are living in their own homes. The attitude that management must act fairly does permeate the by-ways of retirement living. All this helps make some managers age faster or fantasize about their retirement.

Some observers of retirement community living argue that "for-profit communities" are generally more professionally managed than "non-profits." The failure rate of "not-for-profit communities" in California has recently been higher than for "for-profit" communities.

A common management challenge is to maintain full community occupancy in the face of constant resident turnover. The elderly have a nasty habit of dying. Attracting new customers is essential in replacing those departed for the heavenly community. The availability of rooms in the skilled nursing center and the ratio of the retirement community's independent living residents to beds in the skilled center is an important occupancy consideration. Resident demand for skilled nursing beds may occasionally outstrip availability when they are most needed. The community may be forced to send independent living residents to outside skilled nursing facilities. This can be disruptive to a married elderly couple.

Ambiguous comments by marketing employees about their property might cause a retiree to reconsider or postpone moving into that retirement community until a later date. As a result he might die before moving in. He would then be unable to participate in the most powerful retirement experience of his life. A retiree might put away his unsigned retirement community contract for a later review. The following week he is diagnosed with stage-four cancer. Community managements rightly exercise caution in granting residency to seriously disabled applicants. This decision voids the best laid retirement plans.

On the other hand, some people may be close to making a retirement move in a very educated and calculated manner. They have carefully researched their options. Actions in life always have outcomes. In most cases, a retiree will be drawn towards a sound retirement decision. We trust in our new lifestyle.

A RETIRED COUPLE VISITS AN OVERSEAS RETIREMENT COMMUNITY

While on an extended overseas trip, two residents of an American retirement community visited a foreign retirement property. The visit was unplanned. This story recounts an incident they experienced during their visit.

"Marge, it would be interesting to visit a local retirement community while we're staying here."

"What a good idea," she replied. "We've got time on our hands. We could compare a local facility with our own retirement place back in America. The Residents' Marketing Support Committee back home might appreciate the information."

After several inquiries they made an appointment to visit a retirement community considered by locals to be the best in the city they were visiting. They introduced themselves as visitors from America.

During their escorted tour, they walked down a corridor and into the facility's living room. They glanced around.

In a soft voice Marge said to her husband, "Goodness sakes! Do you see those folks slouched in their wheelchairs and lined up along that wall?"

"I sure do," he replied. "It looks like they're all asleep."

"I think they are," she replied.

"We wake them up at 5 pm for dinner," their hostess commented.

"That's very nice," Mary replied.

A short time later.

They thanked the host for the tour and left.

"I'm glad we're returning home on Saturday," said the husband.

"So am I," Mary replied.

"Nothing succeeds like excess."
—Oscar Wilde

PART V
LEGISLATION, LOBBYING AND RETIREMENT COMMUNITIES

SENIORS AND RELATED LEGISLATIVE AFFAIRS

M y concern about retirement equity causes me to periodically change my style of writing. This is another such a moment.

We are a long way from experiencing Japan's aging population dilemmas. This country does look to the USA for new ideas about retirement community living. The impact of Japan's elderly on the country's economic and social affairs is significant. Might we eventually learn from them? Whatever their attitudes, seniors want their social needs and opinions to be heard.

Many supportive organizations coexist alongside continuing care retirement communities. Retirement living is not simply about prompt food service, adequately sized bedrooms, or the provision of transportation for residents. The outside world is very active in retiree thought and action.

It is useful to be reminded that a number of organizations, such as state governments serve retirees in protecting residents' rights and their monetary investments. Legislation has been enacted to overcome perceived arbitrary ownership actions. The State of California has played a role by speaking to the issues of retirement community practices and standards.

No one challenges the fact that retirement community residents have residency rights. The task is to understand why, how, when, or where these rights might or might not be beneficially applied, and interpreted, in relation to a diverse array of institutions. This is where state and local governments have entered into the retirement operation picture. In past years states have periodically enacted legislation affecting the retirement community industry.

In most instances this interface with residents has worked well. Issues and problems occasionally crop up. This includes the need for more effective communications, or the scope of semi-annual resident meeting involving management and the residents. The goal is to create fairer management practices and relationships.

States have continued to promulgate regulations or enact laws that protect the elderly. Some legislators argue for a greater role in retirement community oversight. Others promote the enhancement of social conditions. Still other legislators exclaim, "Keep your hands off the entire retirement business."

Over time, many states have passed legislation that conceptually and concretely supports a retiree's expectations of being . . . . *"endowed by their Creator with certain unalienable Rights, that among these are Life, Liberty and the Pursuit of Happiness."*

California is sensitive to protecting retiree rights. It has legislated on behalf of a general class of retirement facilities referred to as Continuing Care Retirement Communities (CCRCs). An example of supportive state legislation is the California Health and Safety Code, Chapter 10, Division 2. The Code was implemented to ensure CCRC residents would enjoy a greater awareness of proprietors' operations.

Through such actions the State has facilitated greater insight into the quality of community services, and what might be done to make appropriate changes. Legislation has somewhat described community managements' obligations. This includes reducing conflict, respect for residents, selection of residents' representatives, as well as the free and open discussion of retiree issues. Regulations were enacted since some retirement organizations were thought to have acted improperly or arbitrarily. This has motivated States to issue regulations.

CALIFORNIA LEGISLATIVE ACTIONS

By way of introduction, the National Center on Elder Abuse published the following research statistics on elderly abuse.

- 23.4% of substantiated reports of mistreatment of older adults were due to financial exploitation.
- 17% were due to physical abuse.
- 32.5% were due to caregiver neglect.
- The overall reporting of financial exploitation is only 1 in 25 cases.[3]

Retirement communities typically disallow debate on legislative issues within their facilities. Thus some retirees engage

---

[3] National Center on Elderly Abuse. With permission.

directly in political affairs through outside channels, individuals and organizations. They therefore associate with these entities by joining organizations of their choice, paying monthly dues, or making donations to bodies with similar attitudes and causes.

A number of national, state and local entities have championed retirement care and living issues. Others advocate the repudiation of certain healthcare initiatives. All of these establishments serve a watchdog role in upholding the interests of stakeholders in the retirement community sector.

The State of California Welfare and Institutions Code #15630

This section of the Code refers to elderly adult abuse. It includes the following wording.

"California law provides that any person who has assumed full or intermittent responsibility for the care or custody of an elder or dependent adult, whether or not he or she receives compensation, or any elder or dependent adult care custodian, health practitioner, clergy member, or employee of a county adult protective services agency or a local law enforcement agency, is a mandated reporter. Any one of these individuals, who observe or have knowledge of an incident that reasonably appears to be physical abuse, abandonment, abduction, isolation, financial abuse, or neglect, or who is told by an elder or dependent adult that he or she has experienced behavior constituting physical abuse, abandonment, abduction, isolation, financial abuse or neglect, or who reasonably suspects that abuse, must report the known or suspected instance of abuse by telephone immediately or as soon as reasonably practicable, and in writing within two working days, as specified."

The State of California, Health and Safety Code # 1569

This section of the California Code "increases the fines for all elder abuse crimes including fraud, forgery, theft, embezzlement, identify theft and physical abuse. The increases in fines will be dedicated to the Adult Protective Services Agency in the jurisdiction where the crime is prosecuted for the purpose of abuse prevention and investigation. This is a critical and important feature, as Adult Protective Services in most counties remains both underfunded and understaffed. Further, Code 1569 establishes a framework in the financial code for the prevention of fraudulent signature-stamp use. This law is an important bill that will protect older and disabled adults."

ADVOCATING FOR RETIREES

Organizations exist to support many elderly causes, as well as to highlight grievances. Community residents read and hear about the requests and sponsorships being voiced by elderly care advocacy groups. Retirees are periodically urged to support initiatives that combat discriminatory or unfair practices, or the need to close regulatory or legislative gaps. These organizations attempt to influence the legislative process.

Initiating certain public discourses from within a retirement community are frowned on. A number of advocacy organizations communicate directly with residents by using such tools as announcements, mailers and emails. Legislative or social recommendations and actions are continually analyzed and publicized.

The following example of a California advocacy organization initiative is excerpted from a CALCRA association newsletter. It was prepared in the interest of advocating for the State's continuing care retirement community residents.

CALCRA NEWS [4]

California Continuing Care RESIDENTS Association

One-to-One Caregivers in Long-term Care Facilities

"Long-term facilities are increasingly requiring that residents receive and pay for "sitters," also called one-to-one caregivers. To make up for deficient supervision, the facility hires, or requires the resident to hire, a one-to-one caregiver to ensure a person is watching the resident every moment of the day. The costs of a one-to-one caregiver, generally $25 per hour or $600 per day, are, in addition to the facility's basic daily rate, placing enormous and often impossible monetary pressures on residents. In most cases, facilities may not legally require a resident to pay for one-to-one caregivers.

Nursing homes are required by law to provide all services necessary for the resident to maintain or attain the highest level of operation. One of the foremost services a nursing home provides to all residents is protective supervision. If a nursing home cannot effectively supervise a resident it must hire the staff necessary to do so. It cannot delegate its own responsibility to the resident to provide adequate supervision. In short, a nursing home cannot require a resident to pay for

---

[4] CALCRA News: Volume VI, Issue 5, Summer Edition. With permission.
CANHR publication. With permission.

his/her own one-to-one caregiving; in fact it shouldn't even ask.

Assisted living facilities are very different from nursing homes. In addition, facility staffing levels should be monitored to ensure the residents have sufficient staff to meet their needs, and provide basic supervision."

The CALCRA organization works tirelessly to advocate on behalf of continuing care retirement community residents.

We are such stuff as dreams are made on,
and our little life is rounded with a sleep."
—William Shakespeare, The Tempest

PART VI
CONTINUING CARE RETIREMENT
COMMUNTIES AND SKILLED NURSING

"The chain is only as strong as its weakest link."

A GLIMPSE AT SPECIAL CARE

ACCRC resident's wellbeing is assessed relative to the individual's current condition, his ability to cope, his next of kin, facility management, and a physician. A request by management to relocate a resident from independent living to the assisted living facility is known to initiate tension and disagreement. The quality of resident life in independent living is clearly more valued than that of living in skilled nursing. Many residents dislike being relocated, whether voluntarily or involuntary. Skilled nursing is disliked because some perceive it as little removed from hospital living. On occasion, the need to be moved is necessary and even welcomed.

Relocation disputes do crop up. Disagreements must be addressed. Residents have rights. A decision on being relocated to an assisted living facility is usually arrived at by consultations between concerned stakeholders. This protects the rights of residents to remain in their apartments, and not be unilaterally transferred. The security and protection of an individual is important. Action is taken in the best interests of the resident, and other stakeholders.

Skilled nursing facilities are described as.

> "A place of residence for people with difficulties who require constant nursing attention and have significant deficiencies with activities of daily living. Residents include both elderly and younger adults with physical or mental disabilities Residents in a skilled nursing facility may also receive physical, occupational, and other rehabilitative therapies following an accident or illness. Residents may have certain legal rights depending on the location of the facility."[5]

Retirees visit CCRCs, inspect the properties and request information. They consider the alternatives as they unearth the quality and scope of the services they might receive. They talk to community residents, friends, and others. They may consult a lawyer. The younger the lawyer the more unfamiliar he may be with the opportunities and pitfalls of CCRC living. During an expensive consultation, a lawyer may comment "It looks fine to me," or "Their financial condition appears to be satisfactory," or "The community's license seems to be in order." He may add "If you like that place move in," or "No, I don't own their stock," or "Follow your nose." Be nosey!

Retirement communities and healthcare businesses are clearly connected. The quality of comprehensive care and its

---

[5] Wikipedia: The Free Encyclopedia, August 19, 2011.

delivery varies throughout the country. Both are associated with the ability of individuals to claim, pay for, and receive the highest available and affordable levels of care. Some retirees seek retirement facilities that are a few or multiple cuts above a basic retirement care accommodations. Some believe their Social Security and personal savings will fully cover their anticipated retirement costs. They can be wrong about this.

Retirees may not fully recognize that a infirmity may obligate them to spend the remaining two years of their lives in a skilled nursing center. Such a situation might compel them to spend much or all of their life savings on private nursing support.

Private caregiver service is an optional or add-on feature of patient support in a continuing care retirement community. It is expensive and may never be required. Such private care is worth a second thought.

Prospective retirees would do well to investigate the potential cost of retaining private caregivers for a year or two after experiencing a catastrophic physical or cognitive decline. Check the local hourly wage rate for private caregivers. Talk to insurance companies about long-term care insurance. Estimate costs. A retiree may end up talking himself into his immunity from incurring a serious healthcare nursing needs and an accompanying affordability dilemma. Ask yourself if such a financial quandary might happen to you or your spouse.

This scenario of extended caregiving need is not simply a matter of assets, apartment prices, and insurance policies. It amounts to the desired level of compassionate caregiving. An additional consideration is the value of care received for your money. It concerns the ability of a skilled nursing facility, and its caregivers to provide a consistently high level of care in all areas of need. How convinced are you that a particular facility will provide the quality of living and care commensurate with the considerable sum required to reside in that community? In other words, to what extent do you trust your feelings about the quality and value of the care you will receive, in return for the money you would commit to long retirement community life?

Your personal financial planning or residency options may be threatened by unexpected economic and personal circumstances. The stock market may not be on your side. You may be in very serious decline. By considering these elements you will better gauge the implications of longer rather than shorter periods of residency in a skilled nursing center.

CHALLENGES FACING SKILLED NURSING FACILITIES

This narrative and its accompanying counsel are dedicated to Mary Ann

After reading this section the reader might get the impression the author is a senior health care perfectionist, or a vocal and prejudiced critic. He is merely glancing into a rear view mirror as he reflects on the mission and capacities of skilled nursing centers. CCRC marketing departments actively promote the benefits and advantages of their skilled nursing facilities. They have every reason to do so. They espouse their organization's commitment to comprehensive and quality elderly care.

The practice of human caring is a technology woven within an art. Proficiency enters into this scenario. Skillful nursing is a part of the everyday concept of care for the elderly. In a very basic way, *skilled* nursing facilities are variously referred to as nursing care facilities, skilled care facilities, skilled nursing units, and skilled care homes. Most of these nomenclatures contain a key word: *skilled*.

Skilled nursing centers are a key component of the CCRC style of retirement living. These communities strongly differentiate themselves from other community approaches to retirement living. CCRCs are geared to offer retirees an integrated retirement environment. It is very convenient for active residents to benefit from adjacent assisted living, memory support and skilled nursing facilities. Residents can more readily relocate from an active lifestyle to a higher level of needed care. The decision to enter a CCRC depends on the perceived need for reliable physical and mental support, and a desire for health services security.

CCRC standards are primarily the concern of State governments. Government agencies have expressed themselves on appropriate standards for skilled nursing care. These standards are periodically questioned and may not be consistently enforced. CCRCs are a government regulated environment. The quality and extent of care in these facilities are always of concern to staff members, deteriorating patients and their families.

Operating staff excellence in caregiving dramatically influences performance. It is not simply a matter of healthcare technical skills. Administrative excellence in a nursing center is measured in such ways as facility compensation levels, employee selection, training, and staff competencies. Prescribed standards and performance levels must comply with the routine audits of government agencies. Audits may be too infrequent. Or they can be of variable quality. The caliber of performance reviews often varies greatly. The patient has little direct influence over actions that affect employee performance and results. They totally trust the provider.

Patient residency and care in a nursing facility varies from a few days to several years. In this context, managers of nursing centers should remind themselves of their duty to continuously examine the quality of care for patients needing extended periods of care. Invariably, the longer a patient's stay the greater the healthcare challenge. Some patients are unfortunately destined for long confinements that might include extensive periods of disability. In some cases such caregiving becomes palliative. The level of care required by severely challenged patients can bear little similarity to the extent of caregiving required by some short-term residents.

The practices or focus of skilled care offered by a skilled nursing facility may generally be viewed as providing professional, timely, consistent and consistently high levels of caregiving to all patients. Some CCRCs may not provide an ideal level of caregiving with their existing staff and competencies. Yet such facilities do fully meet government staffing requirements. Some nursing facilities find themselves challenged to provide qualified and adequate long-term nursing care for the very debilitated.

In the broad context of such caregiving scenarios, it is interesting to conceptually compare and review two healthcare environments. Caregiving can be scrutinized in two contrasting care provider scenarios. Both require *skilled* employees. They are described as follows.

- *Extended care* provided to continually diminishing patients in a skilled nursing facility by highly qualified professional staff, as well as their entry level staff.
- *Short duration care* provided to critical patients in a hospital's intensive care unit by well qualified professional staff, as well as their entry level staff.

Each of these job categories and environments requires physically and emotionally capable employees. They must both be qualified to do difficult work. They must have "can do" attitudes. All contribute their personal skills, particularly when an intensive care patient receives a high level of professional care from a very qualified and experienced nurse. All positions require responsiveness and patience. Both job areas have similar needs in caregiver attributes and physical capacities.

The relative time span of caregiving is a major difference in the services rendered in these two work environments. The word *skilled* is a common descriptor for both employment environments. Which of the employee levels, in both facilities clearly merits a greater, or lesser *skilled* label, particularly at the entry level of employment? What is the ratio of *skilled* to *custodial* work in each facility? Are they not in reverse orders within these two environments? How might these scenarios affect pay scales? What are equitable wage scales for *skilled* versus *custodial* performers? And then there are relative performance standards.

The term *skilled* reflects certain connotations in the delivery of nursing care. Every employee who helps turn a bedridden patient must have excellent work *skills*, and the ability and competence to do this essential work. Is this simply *custodial* care? Both work environments share *custodial* and *skills* elements. This does not mean that one category should be less relatively *skilled* than the other.

Patient immobility and the decline of bodily functions place increasing and significant demands on both patient and caregiver. The fragility and suffering of a long-term patient can be a test of nursing staff attitudes. It challenges the endurance of a patient's family and friends. How might CCRCs better respond to caregiving employment requirements with the pool of available personnel in the local marketplace? It comes down to income, expenditures, recruiting, pay scales and commitment.

Relatives and patients become apprehensive over discrepancies in the quality of extended patient care. Some patient families and advocacy organizations maintain that managers do not provide consistent round the clock care, or staff scheduling, for the very needy. Some complain about the quality of information transfer from shift to shift. The cause of this may be inadequate and poorly motivated staff, inferior training, turnover rates, or poor attitudes and procedures. Even poor pay.

Nursing care staffs have occasionally received excessive criticism. Caregivers have been cited as the cause of inadequacies in rendering proper care. On the other hand very dedicated staff members have been unfairly criticized.

What are the acceptable and actual levels of employee skills? Simply hiring under-qualified or unsuited staff at affordable wage rates, and then expecting the new hire to learn on the job is inexcusable. How do you assess the relationship of empathy with caring? Leadership and company policies are keys to high performance. Corporate profitability flies in the face of staffing decisions, health care budgets, staff salaries, and organization culture. In addition, employer indifference to employment-for-life attitudes might be scrutinized. Employee terminations must be reasonable. Staff turnover must be managed. How do CCRCs deal with an employee who works in an unsuited environment? These are challenges.

The following ideas are directed at nursing care managers. They include several areas of staffing skills and behaviors that might benefit from training and/or operational attention. They are.

- Responsiveness to urgent patient needs.
- The transfer of patient information between shifts.

- Coping with patient fragility, stress, and frustration.
- Listening skills.
- The need to further improve supervisory skills and practices.
- Recruiting, selection against rigorous standards,
- Reduction in staff turnover.

How responsive is management to needed improvement? Employee sourcing and nepotism might be issues. There is the question of language and work culture. The quality of care may be affected by a lack of English language skills and comprehension. The operating culture may need to be studied and better defined.

The narrative has drifted towards employee skills competencies.

In the midst of all this is the genuineness of those who give, and those who receive. Many heroic patients and their dedicated caregivers have willingly crossed the thresholds of skilled nursing centers throughout the country. They share a spirit of mutual sensitivity and understanding. God Bless them all!

In a macro sense, these care issues cannot be blithely referred to as healthcare socialism or free enterprise approaches to caring. Neither should they be characterized by the expression "If you don't like it here go try the United Kingdom, Canada, or New Zealand." As a whole, continuing care retirement communities in the USA generally compare more favorably against overseas settings. The argument is simply the soundest application of ethics, business principles, policy, behaviors and practices to a critical segment of the United State's healthcare industry.

"Contemplation of life after retirement and life after death can help you deal with contemporary challenges."
—Russell M. Nelson

PART VII
RETIREE HAPPENINGS IN THE OUTSIDE WORLD

IN-STORE SHOPPING CARTS FOR THE DISABLED

The following are written and verbal exchanges about in-store disabled shopper carts at a large local retail store. It begins with a letter to Mr. Douglas McTavish, President of Costless Wholesale Stores.

Dear Sir,

I am writing you about the lack of disabled person carts in your large store, located near my retirement community. Many elderly residents shop there. In fact, our community occasionally runs a shopping bus for its residents to your store. Only three carts are available for disabled shoppers. This is an insufficient number considering the many elderly shoppers who visit your store. You may be inadvertently turning elderly customers away from your store. I would appreciate hearing from you. A nearby WalSale Store, of equal size, has five carts. Please consider adding three more carts in your store.

Sincerely,

John DeVilbis

The following reply was received from Mr. McTavish.

Dear Mr. DeVilbis,

We appreciate your letter regarding carts for the disabled. We are very sensitive to the needs of our shoppers. This is why we provide carts in all our stores. I am sending a copy of this correspondence to Mr. Jonathan Sprite the Store Manager, for further action. I assure you he will examine ways to improve our services for the disabled shoppers. We value your business.

Sincerely,

Douglas McTavish,

President, Costless Wholesale Stores

A face-to-face conversation between Mr. DeVilbis and Mr. Sprite, the store manager, eventually took place. It proceeded as follows.

"Good afternoon, sir. I am John DeVilbis, a resident in a large retirement community near your warehouse. May we chat about the number of carts for disabled persons in your store? Three carts are inadequate for the volume of customers who trade at your store. As you may know, carts are often unavailable. Did you see a copy of my letter to your president and his reply?"

Mr. Sprite replied.

"Good morning, sir. Thanks for dropping by. I did receive a copy of his letter. Company policy allows me to budget three carts for my store. We therefore have three carts here. I appreciate your concern. We'll look into this matter again. Thanks for bringing this subject to our attention. We always want to hear from our customers."

Six months later only three carts continued to be available at the Costless store.

COUNTING ON A SECURE RETIREMENT INVESTMENT

Economic conditions affect retirement communities. The commitment to provide residents with a high level of care remains in force until the community owner's last invoice is received and remains unpaid. The national real-estate market and other economic conditions impact unit sales. Business plans are modified. Rumors about retirement firms and financial transactions circulate and escalate.

The following information was widely publicized within the retirement community industry. It concerned retirement property ownership and management.

.... Rumors abound that this company is facing bankruptcy. Attempts to sell have been energetic, yet closely guarded. Some information has surfaced. The sale of the property is based on the disposal of all facilities and the job security of their management employees. Several large corporations have shown an interest in purchasing this business. A possible arrangement is being handled by a Los Angeles company ....

Obviously someone had an agenda or an axe to grind. Nothing earth-shattering occurred immediately after this announcement. The official management response was, "There are no plans to sell these retirement communities." Residents care about what happened. Persistent research might have further clarified this development.

There is constant activity in the retirement community investment market. Rumors, studies, and negotiations thrive. Real Estate Investment Trusts (REITs) are principal investment players in retirement property investing. Their managers are constantly on the lookout for business opportunities, at the right time and cost. A slow economy increases selectivity among decision makers. Financial positions and management are at a premium, whether the focus is on assisted living or continuing care retirement communities. REITs aggressively seek the most attractive properties in a shifting economic environment, whether they are independent living or memory support. The hunt for acquisitions goes on. Recognition of the baby boomer phenomenon and its impact on retirement community dealings play an important part in successful planning.

As a REIT manager stated, "We compete with each other. Money is made through the right relationships and contacts." The marketplace is competitive. Financial condition, turnover, and occupancy rates are continually reviewed. Resident attitudes are less frequently scrutinized.

Recessions are anathema to retirement property owners. These adverse conditions can trigger Chapter 11 filings. This stirs up the marketplace and disturbs complacency. Some retirement community property owners may simply tire of the competition. Others are tempted to search elsewhere for their capital gains. Strategic plans are rewritten. A property owner may elect to sell his investment. The good news is that government legislation may, to an extent, shield a resident from feelings of insecurity, or help assuage his concern. It varies by state.

Industry consolidation may become increasingly prevalent, and present itself as a promising opportunity to resolve financial uncertainty. If this strategy played out, the retirement industry might end up with a few big names, and even resemble the hotel industry. A CCRC can be envisioned as an extension of Caesar's Palace in Las Vegas. A lavish retirement community on the Strip might be welcomed. This would eliminate monthly bus rides by residents to enjoy a casino.

Marketing strategies change. An enterprising executive might decide to expand his retirement community operations to include funeral parlors. This is known as vertical integration, or one-stop shopping. Might crematories and wedding chapels be too far off?

DISCONTINUITY IN RETIREMENT COMMUNITY LIVING

Following rumors of a change in ownership, nothing was heard from the retirement community owners. Residents of one of their operations did pay attention to the continued silence. Had their stationary cruise fleet set a new course into deep fog and uncharted waters? Was there clear sailing? The ship's captain must be trusted when it comes to preventing the ship from floundering.

An announcement was eventually made. The owners said they might well dispose of all their retirement properties. The official word, couched in legally approved prose was that the company could not speculate or comment on published and rumored announcements. They asserted that an exploratory sales mission must be carried out with complete discretion. This was understandable, and it robustly stoked the rumor mill.

The residents anticipated the announcement of a resident briefing to explain corporate action, or inaction. Meanwhile, they now had another breakfast topic. The discussions matched the intensity of resident speculation about annual fee increases.

A resident meeting with management was scheduled. Management stated they did not intend to dispose of any properties. They again reiterated that their business planning activities required discretion on their part. The company stated they planned to continue examining opportunities to diversify their business. A resident began searching the national press for more news. Nobody lost much sleep. Some residents simply reverted to worrying about their health, or that of their dogs.

Six months later the story circulated that all the company's retirement properties had been sold to a New York REIT. What happens next? Keep your ears close to the ground.

CALL YOUR PHONE COMPANY TO ACCESS TO HEAVEN AND HELL

Hassles happen in our external world. A common consumer ruckus is caused by organizations that try to improve their operating efficiency through recorded customer call response techniques. They do this by connecting consumers to pre-recorded telephone instructions. A customer can get annoyed by these ad nauseam practices. The elderly can become aggravated.

A retiree called his telephone company to get billing information. He dialed their phone number. The call went something like this.

A recorded message announced,
"Good morning. Thank you for calling. I hope you're having a nice day. We want to help you."
The message continued, "I can help you. But first I need to get some information. What is your telephone number?"
He gave his phone number.
It then asked, "What is your full home address?"
He responded.
The voice requested, "What are the last four numbers of your social?"
He carefully replied.
It then asked, "If you do not wish to be recorded, press 1."

He did not press 1.

The voice continued, "If you're calling about your cell phone, press 1. If you are calling about your home phone, press 2."

He pressed 2.

The voice proceeded,

"If you are calling about billing, press 1."

"If you are calling about technical service, press 2."

"If you are calling about repair scheduling, press 3."

"If you are calling about discontinuation of service, press 4."

"If you are calling about new service, press 5."

"If you are calling about suspension of service, press 6."

"If you are calling about new cell phone service, press 7."

"If you are calling about reinstating your service, press 8."

"If you are calling about office hours, press 9."

"If you are calling about a problem on the line, press 10."

"If you are calling about an unpaid bill, press 11."

"If you are calling about our specials, press 12."

"If you are calling about another subject, press 13."

He pressed 13 and another recorded voice said,

"If you have reached this extension in error, press 1."

"If you have not reached this number in error, press 2."

He pressed 2.

The voice proceeded,

"Our office hours are Monday through Friday from 9 am to 5 pm.

We are currently closed. Please call back or press 1 for further help. Thank you for your patience."

He did not press 1.

He angrily pressed 2 and heard a recorded voice,

"Good morning! This is Heaven speaking. May we help you?"

He realized he was speaking to a recorded celestial voice.

The voice added, "We are sorry, but God is not available right now."

"If you wish to leave a message for God, press 1."

"If you wish to speak to Saint Peter, press 2."
"If you wish to speak to Saint Paul, press 3."
"If you have a biblical question, press 4."
"If you have a spiritual question, press 5."
"If you wish to speak to one of our angels about your transgressions, press 6."
"If you wish to speak to an angel on any other topic, press 7."
"If you wish to leave a message about your sins, press 8."
All he needed was an answer about his phone bill, so he gave up on this ritual. He haphazardly punched 10.
A scratchy voice answered,
"Thank you for holding. If you wish to speak to the Devil, press 1."
"If you wish to speak to Napoleon Bonaparte, press 2."
"If you wish to talk to Joseph Stalin. press 3."
"If you wish to leave us a short message, press 4."
"If you wish to seek penitence, you have reached the wrong number."
"If you have reached the wrong number, you may now hang up."
He knew he had the wrong number and extension.
He hung up.
Heaven, Hell, and the phone company can wait until after his afternoon nap.

Young folks tolerate these inconveniences more so than seniors. This telephone answering practice has yet to be embedded into the elderly culture.

The phone caller realized that both Heaven and Hell have now succumbed to a recorded telephone answering program. There is a moral to this story. If you want to conveniently raise "Heaven or Hell," phone your phone company.

DISJOINTED MEDICAL ATTENTION

L ife's aggravations come in many shapes and sizes. The elderly can get frustrated when dealing with the medical profession. Healthcare and seniors are synonymous. Seniors wholeheartedly depend on good medical care. The quality of healthcare delivery occasionally falls short of its target. When that happens a senior is disappointed. Many lack the energy to complain.

This story begins with a phone call involving a large medical center. A recorded message is heard as a caller patiently waits for an operator to respond. Recordings include such announcements as, "Every day we bring the latest medical discoveries to you . . . . We are nationally recognized as a leading medical provider . . . . We are training the medical personnel of the future." This is known as captive audience marketing, with the added joy of recorded rock music in the background.

The phone call proceeded . . . . He heard a recorded voice that led him through a programmed sequence of questions. Five minutes later he reached a live operator.

"Good morning, sir. May I help you?" asked the medical center's telephone operator.

"Yes you may," replied the caller. "Several medical tests were performed on me recently and I need the results. I've not heard from my doctor's office."

"Oh! I'm sorry to hear that. Let me see what I can do about it. Please give me more information about the tests, and the doctor involved."

He gave details.

The operator added, "Yes, I see from your records that no one has contacted you. I'll send the nurse a message. She will be in touch with you right away."

"Thank you," he replied, and hung up.

He did not receive the test results.

A FEW DAYS LATER . . . .

He arrived at his doctor's office.

The doctor asked him, "Did you get your test results? I don't see anything in your file."

He replied, "No, Doctor, I talked to the medical office about that and haven't heard back."

"Why don't I call their office to find out what's going on?"

"Fine," he answered.

The doctor called and informed him, "The medical office will call you later today and give you your test results."

He thanked the doctor and left.

Two days later he had not received his test results.

A FEW MORE DAYS LATER . . . .

He visited the MRI facility at a medical center to get an MRI with contrast. The MRI nurse asked him about his kidney function. She wanted to be sure his kidneys would not be stressed by a contrast injection. She suggested the patient call the nephrology office and ask them to give him the needed test information on the phone, or have the nurse immediately fax the data to the MRI laboratory. The MRI staff would then have the needed test numbers.

He called the doctor's office and explained his situation. The nurse responded.

"I'm sorry sir. We cannot give you this information over the phone. You need to sign a release form. We prefer you give us notice so we can provide this information."

He replied, "I'm the patient and we're waiting to get started on an MRI. I only need two readings."

The nurse replied, "I'm sorry, those are the rules. If you want your test data immediately you'll have to ask the MRI facility staff to conduct their own blood test."

"Thank you," he said.

"What do we do now?" he asked the MRI nurse.

A brief discussion ensued.

She eventually said, "We can do the test here. Social Security may not reimburse the cost."

"I didn't know that."

The nurse replied, "You will be charged $35 if Social Security does not reimburse you."

He replied, "Let's go ahead."

AND A FEW DAYS LATER . . . .

"This is the Medical Clinic. May I help you?"

"Yes, I want to come in to get a booster injection from the doctor's nurse. This injection is due today."

"We can make arrangements to get that done," said the operator. "You must make an appointment."

He again called for an appointment and got involved in the center's security clearance process.

"What is your full name?"

"What is your social security number?"

"What is your complete address?"

"What is your phone number?"

"Has your insurance coverage changed?"

And so on . . . .

THE CONE OF SILENCE WAS ULTIMATELY REMOVED

A live operator finally came on the line and said, "I'll have to call the doctor to set up your injection."
"You don't need to contact the doctor. He's already scheduled two consecutive booster injections for me."
"I still have to contact the doctor for his approval," she replied.
He replied, "All I need is to have someone schedule an appointment for my injection."
"We have to set this up with the doctor."
"But it's already arranged," he replied.
"We must contact the doctor."
"Please put me through to the doctor's nurse," he asked.
She transferred him.
The line was busy.
"Please leave a message for the nurse," said a recorded voice.
Irritation swept over him.
He hung up feeling very frustrated.

A WEIGHTY MEDICAL DIAGNOSIS

Enabling a patient to interpret a doctor's diagnosis sometimes requires an MD degree. The following determination made perfect sense to a patient after she had carefully consulted a medical dictionary and spoken to a doctor acquaintance. The patient eventually understood the doctors' medical diagnosis. He did have gout.

JOHN SEMETT, MD
5786 Wallace Way

July 8th.

Mr. Oliver Jenkins. Patient # 8593.
187 State Street
Beaumont, OR 47588

Dear Mr. Jenkins,

I am forwarding the results of recent X-rays taken of your left foot. You complained that your foot is paining you. Please note the doctor's report below.

X-RAY OF FOOT, LEFT SIDE

CONDITIONS:

Clinical history: Foot metatarsal pain.
Comparative studies: None available.
Technique: Three views of the left foot.

FINDINGS:

There is periosteal reaction along the shafts of the second through fifth metatarsals, with somewhat nodular appearance. Periosteal reaction along the fourth minute tarsal shaft is more fusiform and continuous appearing. There is no significant endosteal sclerosis to suggest an entity such as melorheostosis. No acute fracture or malalignment is seen. Joint spaces are preserved. Soft tissues are unremarkable.

IMPRESSION:

Periosteal reaction along the shafts of the second through fifth metatarsals with nodular appearance. Differential considerations include causes of diffuse periostitis such as hypertrophic osteoarthropathy. Stress reaction is considered less likely given the multinodular appearance.

No stress is seen. I think the likely explanation for the reactive change is an episode of gout.

(Signed)

John Semmel

That's what gout is about!

ELDERLY FRAUD

The phone rang in the living room of an elderly resident. She switched her television to mute, and answered on the fourth ring. She heard an unfamiliar voice on the line.

"Hello!"

"Hello Grandma. This is Frank, your grandson. Can you hear me? It's Frank!"

"I can hear you, dear. How are you? Your voice sounds strange."

"It's me, Grandma Ruth. I'll speak a little more clearly."

"You still sound strange to me, Frank. Do you have a cold?"

"Yes, I do have a bad one. I hope you can hear me OK. We have a bad connection."

"Yes, it is a poor connection. Mom sends you her love. As you know, she's in New York right now."

"Yes I know. Are you at home?"

"No, I'm in Memphis, Tennessee."

"What in the world are you doing there? Your voice still sounds a little strange to me, dear."

"I'll speak up."

"What are you doing in Memphis?"

"I was hurt in a car accident earlier today, Grandma."

"That's terrible, Frank. What exactly happened? Where are you right now?"

"I was blindsided by a taxi at an intersection. I'm at Memorial Hospital in downtown Memphis."

"I broke my left leg below the knee. I'm now feeling a little better."

"It's good to hear you're not seriously hurt. Did you call your mother?"

"I tried to but couldn't get through."

"So who's looking after you right now, poor boy?"

"I'm on my own and need your help."

"You know I'll always help you all I can."

"I need fifteen hundred dollars to pay for my hospital expenses. Would you please send me money right away. I want to get discharged from the hospital as soon as possible. I really need the money."

"Can't it wait until you can talk to your mother?"

"No, Grandma, I need to get home. I really want to check out and get home."

"I understand. How can I help you right now?"

"Thanks, Grandma. Here's what you need to do. Go to your computer. Sign in to your bank account and make a transfer from your account to mine. Just make a note of my bank account information."

He gave her his bank account information.

"I'll wait on the phone."

"Thank you. Frank, I made a note of the checking account information. I'm headed for the computer right now. I didn't shut it down. It's always good to hear from you. I'm glad to help you. Frank it won't take me more than a couple of minutes to send you the money. Do you mind holding on? I'll be back on the line as soon as I can."

"No problem Grandma. I'll wait."

After completing the transaction she came back on the phone.

"The transaction went through. Is there anything else I can do for you?"

"No, Grandma, that's all for now. Thank you so much."

"Look after yourself, Frank. Let me know if I can help. I love you."

The voice Grandma heard was not that of her grandson Frank. It was a professional scammer who successfully preys on the elderly. This is just one of the ways a senior can be victimized.

MAKING AIRLINE RESERVATIONS ON THE PHONE MEANS PRESSING TOO MANY NUMBERS ON A KEYPAD

A frustrating phone conversation can occur when you phone an airline to make a reservation. The process can intrude on your tranquility. It can also limit your spare time.

He decided to visit an out-of-town relative, so he phoned an airline to make a reservation. In the old days the customer was directly connected to a living and helpful agent. Such calls were very often positive.

The following is another frustrating time-waster. It details a conversation with an airline reservations agent. After dialing he heard a recorded message. The phone call proceeded as follows.

"Due to high call volume we encourage you call us later. Or you may remain on the line."
He waited.
"Thank you for calling. What is your mileage number? If you don't have your mileage number press 1."
The call continued.
"I'm sorry, I didn't understand that. Please reply by entering your numbers on the keypad, or say the numbers after the tone."
The voice continued,
"Is your call about an old reservation, or do you wish to make a new reservation?"
"Do you wish to make a one-way or a round-trip reservation?"
"Tell me, what is your departure city?"
"I need to know the city and state you wish to fly to?"
"I need to know if this is for award travel."
"If it's for award travel, press 1. If it's not for award travel, press 2."
"I need to know if this is a reservation for your own travel only, or are there other travelers?"
Press 1 if this is for your travel only."

"Press 2 if this is for more than one traveler."
He pressed the wrong number in error.
A recorded voice asked, "If you want to start from the top again press 1."
He pressed 1.
The voice continued,
"Let me ask you, do you wish to make a reservation or are you calling for another reason?"
"What is your date of departure?"
His reply was, "May 15th."

This went on until he had registered the desired flight number and departure information. He yearned for a live and helpful agent. There and then he decided to talk to a real living agent. He eventually accessed one.

He learned he was connected to a reservations agent located in Chicago, Illinois. Every day, this ticket agent flies directly from her home in Delhi, India to her workplace at the airline's Chicago reservations office. Her daily flight booking is made for her by a live and helpful ticket agent located in the airline's Chicago office. Each day this proficient Chicago agent promptly issues round trip advanced ticketing to the New Delhi Agent for her daily personal travel to and from Chicago.

"As I grow older, I pay less attention to what men say.
I just watch what they do."
—Andrew Carnegie

PART VIII
ADJUSTING TO A RETIREMENT COMMUNITY ENVIRONMENT
Things that Happen Most of the Time

R etirees do cogitate. They want to know how quickly they
will adjust to retirement community living. They speculate
on how quickly they will adapt to this lifestyle. Retirees worry
about the vagaries of retirement community living and its environment. They then reflect on the things they learned to like
and dislike after having moved in. Residents eventually find
their expectations were correct, or perhaps imperfect. They
are versatile and find ways to adapt to their new way of living.

ADJUSTING

R elocating to a CCRC demands noteworthy adjustments.
To some a rearrangement of lifestyle may simply be

perceived as another lifetime inconvenience. Being elderly certainly adds stress to any relocation. Moving disrupts habits, strains patience and upsets tranquility. Residents survive. Few newcomers become severely aggravated with this self-imposed transformation. They never get insufferable.

As a rule, relatively smooth transitions are the outcome of relocating to a retirement community. Dead tiredness is inevitable. The move is never straightforward. Retirement community managements do their best to ensure orderly transitions.

Facility managements do not check on the criminal record of prospective residents. This is always done with employment applicants. They do carefully interview prospective retirees; check their financial resources, and the condition of their health. Becoming the ward of a community is an embarrassment to all. Having a number of long stay 100 year old residents in a CCRC will generate prolonged euphoria. It is a minor source of management concern about apartment turnover estimates and cash flow.

The social vicissitudes of old age become more evident to retirees as they seriously implement their relocation plans. This and the entry fee are two reasons why a large number of the elderly wish to remain in their own homes. They may alternatively elect to move into an assisted living complex.

Some individual are retiring in their ways and adapt more slowly. Behavior modification is a consideration in the transition process. Most residents adapt swiftly and integrate successfully. New residents quickly familiarize themselves with the location of the dining room, and that facility buses leave promptly from the north entrance. They discover where to get their blood pressure checked. They understand that making new friends is exciting and uncomplicated.

In time, an affable new resident might become a member of the CCRC's rumor mill. Some new residents may eventually attain even greater community status by being recognized as the initiator of topics for all to gossip about. A very gabby resident may eventually advance to the level of architect of titillating community stories. This progression is never calculated to promote nastiness, simply as a way to avoid becoming bored.

As time goes on the extent and nature of resident irritations, and negative feelings may arise. Criticisms about the facility, the managers, and their departments can increase. Food is a lightning rod of criticism. Some residents thrive on castigating the Managing Director. All is fair in love and retirement community living.

Following relocation into a community, a resident's initial perceptions of their new lifestyle will be verified, and their opinions are proven or disproven. Humans are fundamentally social in nature. Making a firm decision to get along is the surest answer to maintaining a tranquil way of living.

Getting along means accepting the fact that community managers have the residents' interests at heart. It means recognizing that skilled nursing care managers have a fix on complex caring challenges, and do their best to enhance a demanding healthcare environment. It means accepting the fact that a neighbor is not really that opinionated.

Selecting a lifestyle that integrates with established community policies may not be a preferred approach for some. Regardless, an increasingly sheltered lifestyle will eventually be required as a retiree becomes further incapacitated.

A strong need for personal privacy may not allow heavy socializing. Some residents participate less actively in internally organized activities. They favor social interaction with the outside world. Outside entertainment may be more importance than happy hours and community organized programs. Relatives drop by to check on how things are going. These visits are reciprocated. Some residents do not relish the closeness of community living. Residents are openly encouraged to spend their preferred lives in retirement bliss.

Transitioning and adaptability are ingredients of elderly flexibility. Retirees maintain steadfastness in their ways. The testing of adaptability is a part of life, and inevitably reoccurs. As residents age they will again be required to make relocation decisions, such as moving to a higher level of personal care. Health limitations are more manifested as time goes on. Wellbeing can deteriorate as mental acuity diminishes. Shifting needs befall us, and herald another phase of our lives.

TWENTY ASSORTED BIASES

The following is my personal list of water-cooler retirement topics. If your retirement community does not have a water cooler, try your fitness room. These are aspects of retirement life that have made strong impressions on this author.

I'M KEEN ON	**I'M NOT KEEN ON**
Clare	Bingo
Church	Flat tires
Good wine	Tardiness
Good health	Cloudy days
Summertime	Night driving
Camano Island	Nosey people
The Navy League	Rationalizing
My independence	Cold weather
I can still drive my car	Blocked toilets

"We haven't gone this far because we're made of sugar candy." [6]
—Winston S. Churchill

SOME GOOD AND NOT SO GOOD IMPRESSIONS OF CCRC LIVING

In a quiet moment the writer developed two lists about CCRC living. They identify a number of perceived advantages and disadvantages of this retirement lifestyle. Each list might interest other retirees, including some unfamiliar with CCRCs. They might interest existing residents of a retirement community. They are subjective and stem from many years in a community.

SOME PERCEIVED ADVANTAGES OF CCRC LIVING

Physical and emotional security.

Close access to medical facilities.

You are among a group of elderly folks who often share similar values.

New move-in friends.

Diverse resident backgrounds.

Opportunities to enthusiastically complain.

Opportunities to suggest things.

Medical attention is available at the 24 hour nurses center.

You have a wide choice of friends.

Independence.

Residents who care.

Visits to family and visits by family.

Dignity.

Respect.

Comfort.

Companionship.

---

[6] Winston S. Churchill: New York City speech after /Pearl Harbor, September, 1941.

Fairness and integrity.
Trust.
Afternoon tea with an opportunity to gab, and possibly reinvent the community wheel.
The staff usually listens.
Weekly housekeeping service.
You can "lock up your apartment and take off."
You do not have to get involved in community activities.
You never have to use your kitchen oven unless you opt to.
Covered car parking.

Participating in happy hours.
A variety of volunteer activities.
The Internet.
A supportive staff.
Partying with friends.
The staff works hard.
Organized activities and programs.
Easy access to assisted living and skilled care.
Transportation to off-site locations.
Close access to stores.

SOME PERCEIVED DISADVANTAGES OF CCRC LIVING

A small sacrifice of privacy.
The inevitable annual fee increase.
Staff turnover.
A very few residents who bother you.
There are too many elderly folks around.
Bureaucracy.
Sloppy maintenance work.
Weekends.
No relatives live close by.
Things are occasionally ordained.

You sometimes forget what day it is.
Management rationalizations.
Loneliness.
My church is a long drive away.
Friends die too frequently.
Junk mail.
Smelly garbage chutes.
Precious little rain.
The norovirus.

"All right then. If you stop telling residents I have the norovirus,
I'll quit telling them you have Alzheimer's."

RETIREE LAMENTS

O ld age introduces new settings and experiences that con-
front us all. Strangers occasionally take advantage of the
elderly. Nevertheless, seniors are usually well respected and
properly treated. Some experiences do disturb a condition of
equilibrium. Here are examples that might cause unease.

Doctors who tend to over-medicate.
Medical errors and sloppiness.
Expensive medications.
Young folks who decline to give up their seats to
the elderly.
Private nurses who fall asleep on the job.
Folks who steal your ideas.
Over salted food.
Small yappy dogs.
Stores that have an insufficient number of electric
carts for the disabled.
Falling down.
Getting up.
The rare staff member who has argued with a
resident.
People who try to scam you.
Folks who do not smile, or greet you warmly.
Long stairways.
Steep streets.
Marketing oversell.
Family indifference.

Language and comprehension differences.
The gradual attrition of retirement community services and benefits.
Cancellation of a driving license.
Recorded commercial telephone calls.
Drivers who honk at you.
Old ladies who wink at old men.
Lack of principle.
Self-pity.
Pain.
Losing friends.
Bleeding.
Waiting on phone calls.
Losing your cane or hat.

*"Inside every older person is a younger person
wondering what has happened."*
—Jennifer Yane

PART IX
ROMANCE AND RETIREMENT COMMUNITIES

A CAUTIOUS OVERVIEW

The next vignettes include tongue-in-cheek characterizations of retirement community romances, such as they may occur. It also contains commentaries about warm, loving, and personal relationships.

Candid portrayals of romances are unmentioned in community marketing brochures. Management will only describe romantic settings in hushed tones. After all, the elderly rarely move into a retirement community to become romantically attached. That does not mean a retiree or two will not change his mind about another romance. It has happened. On the other hand some retirees simply maintain romantic involvements within their hearts. They pine for their spouses.

In a more practical way, the following is sensible advice for newly relocated retirement community residents. This information was previously published in a retirement magazine. The issue quickly became a collector's item.

ADVICE BY MANAGEMENT TO NEW RESIDENTS

We have nothing against dating in our retirement community.

JUST DO NOT KISS TOO MUCH IN PUBLIC!

You may wonder if sex is ever discussed hereabouts?

Well it is!

Sex is seldom discussed in the dining room,

only in the abstract

and rather infrequently by female residents.

ELDERLY ROMANCES HAVE THEIR TWISTS AND TURNS

Some conversation topics must be avoided by the CCRC resident and are never mentioned in a resident handbook. Conversation topics in a retirement facility must involve safe social topics. Discussion outcomes vary and depend on the intensity of mutual feelings. The passion of some conversations can be quite intense.

Three conversational topics must be handled carefully. Avoid careless and indiscreet chatter about party politics, the dogmas of religions and the reasons for the breakup of a stressful relationship. In some quarters resident tranquility hits the rocks around election time. Salvation issues are best left to inner thoughts or between adherents of the same faith, or no faith at all. Prudence is needed when taking sides on the intricacies of romance. On the other hand some individuals forever take issue over the most mundane topics.

A retiree once made the profound statement, during a happy hour that the seeds of loving affection remain alive for 10 days after a person is buried. No one argued with this assertion although a resident did question the research methodology.

Resident handbooks have never established age limits on prolonged or fleeting companionships. They never will. This may be due to the strict minimum age requirements governing entry into a retirement community. It is always assumed there are no maximum age limits. Neither have they established any parameters for dalliances.

Some social statements are simply poor form, such as the assertion that men should never expect sex before the fourth or fifth date. This suggestion would not exemplify resident morality, and would surely refer to other surroundings than retirement communities. There is a strong conviction that discussing entrapment is simply very bad form, or that cohabitation comments must be delicately maneuvered around.

It is an exaggeration to suggest that romantic encounters are a constant part of retirement community life. Some simply live in hope. A retiree or two may fantasize too much. Residents are on safe ground when suggesting that risk-averse residents avoid the hazards of community romance. Personal inclinations may simply extend to thinking about it all. Sheer envy, loyalty, or a sorrowful past can influence personal attitudes and motivation. Being jilted is simply unheard of.

The drive for amity and a partnership can stimulate energy levels. Social linkages may eventually range from limited social associations to elopement. The latter is resoundingly admired, even by a loser in the chase. Matrimony is the retirement community's ultimate romantic behavior. The resulting ceremony surpasses Valentine's Day festivities in the community.

Rumors thrive. This is a cottage industry. Risqué topics titillate residents. Group curiosity and chatter are unavoidable. Here is a sampling of questions often asked during community breakfasts.

"What dalliances are happening these days?"
"Are they really emotionally attracted to each other?"
"That new resident looks like a great conquest for someone!"
"Is it simply fascination or a warm and developing friendship?"
"Has anyone ever seen them kissing?"
"On the lips? Really?"
"Oh, well."
"When do you think that romance will break up?"
"Why do you say that?"
"Who knows?"
"How long will it take Mr. Jones to recover from that experience?
"Did you really hear them squabbling?"

On it goes. Scuttlebutt is never published in weekly news bulletins.

New residents, on joining a retirement community, never overtly request information about romantic opportunities. In fact it is not even on their minds. They would be told the opportunities are very rare.

Lectures about romance in a community are very rarely scheduled. Romantic movies are shown all the time. The geriatrics department of a leading university prepared an entertaining lecture on "Elderly Genders and Sexual Behavior." Several local retirement communities never did schedule this intriguing presentation for their residents. The event would have sold out. They felt too many residents would have blushed.

Flirtation tactics are usually left to one's intuition. Jealousies can be aggravating to management, and are notable for their rarity. They can be particularly amusing and receive hushed comments. It is incorrect to suggest romantic interludes flourish in June and wane at Federal Tax time. Romantic associations rarely occur in a skilled care center. The very few that have occurred there were triggered by mistaken identity, or complete forgetfulness. Pangs of conscience are rare.

Managements attempt to keep aloof of all these commotions. They do informally hold their ears to the ground. Romantic interludes are periodically commented on at staff meetings. Statements are typically made after a solemn recollection about residents who have recently died. Executive Directors always limit group speculation, conjecture or the intensity of discussions.

CARING MEANS BREAKING BREAD TOGETHER

The elderly couple always came down to eat dinner at 5:30 pm. He slowly wheeled her into the dining room. The dining room hostess greeted them warmly. They were guided to a table for two at the far corner of the room. She always asked about their health and received an identical response. It always came from him, "Just great, thank you, just great."

With some effort, she was eased out of her wheelchair and transferred to a dining room chair. She always smiled weakly after being comfortably seated. He unfolded a napkin and placed it round her neck. He handed her a menu. The menu did not interest her. So he read her the menu items and asked what she wanted to order. She simply smiled. Her husband always ordered for both of them.

He moved on to some casual talk. Her replies were infrequent and unclear. If you looked at her hands, you would see they were clenched at her sides. She was unable to use the utensils placed in front of her. Over time he had learned to expertly feed her.

When their food arrived he cut hers into small pieces and carefully fed her using small spoonfuls. She found it difficult to swallow each mouthful. So she simply kept the food in her mouth a little longer. Occasionally he put too much food on the spoon. It spilled onto her lap. Things occasionally got messy.

Eating dinner took time. He fed himself while he fed her. He developed the bad habit of gulping down his own dinner. She relished desserts. They both enjoyed coffee at the end of their meal. Her husband invariably asked her if she had eaten well.

During dinner they smiled at everyone. Residents occasionally dropped by their table to chat and to wish the couple well.

A resident occasionally commented she should be moved to the assisted living center. She was eventually relocated there.

They now eat dinner together in the assisted living dining room. He continues to feed her tenderly and methodically. After dinner he occasionally forgets to remove the napkin from around her neck. She does not care. He dutifully shifts her into the wheelchair. She is then slowly wheeled out of the dining room. She does not care about the formalities of mealtime. Punctuality and menus mean little to her. They smile and wave at the other diners while they exit the dining room.

TWO VERY DISSIMILAR BUDDIES

Dog (Noun): *"A domestic carnivorous animal with a long muzzle, fur coat and a long fur-covered tail, and whose characteristic call is a bark."*[7]

This is a story about man's best friend and retirement living. Butch was a retired dog who lived with his 94-year-old owner. What happened that day was sudden and peaceful. The event was a shock that left his owner feeling much lonelier. The dog died early one morning. The owner had deep feelings about that. He felt much sorrow.

---

[7] Encarta Dictionary: English/North American Edition.

Butch had been the thirteen-year-old canine companion of a retired investment banker from Chicago. Their togetherness grew after his wife died, and increased as time went on. He eventually developed a stronger affection towards Butch than anyone else in his community. His life was committed to a small Scottish terrier.

The owner had no remaining close relatives. He lived a secluded life in a large, comfortable, three-bedroom retirement community apartment. Remaining family members never visited. The two guest bedrooms in his apartment always remained empty. He had outlived most of his friends. He read or watched television. He rarely felt bored. The old man simply fussed over Butch and gave him all his loving attention.

The dog received attentive caring, as every dog must in a retirement community. This meant that Butch received the best medical care. The owner insisted that Butch would receive dog care equaling people care. His pet did not care much one way or another.

It was amazing how this dog and his master had integrated their routines. They both knew exactly when their daily walks would occur. They intuitively knew the park they always visited, and how far they would walk along its trails. Taking afternoon walks was a daily necessity.

Some time ago the motto of his community was changed to read, "It's a place where you can add many years to your life." He was sure this motto also applied to residents' dogs. Life in the retirement community would definitely add years to a dog's life. He once suggested to management that their future advertisements include references to dogs, and include dog pictures. They politely declined.

Butch had a sophisticated girlfriend. Her name was Diedre. She could easily have won a community dog beauty contest. She did not look at all like her owner. Diedre lived the good life. She was playful and full of happiness, except when she growled at that fierce-looking resident who always growled back. She was also very attractive with long curly dark hair and big brown eyes. Bright red nail polish was regularly applied to Deidre's well-manicured nails. This dog was a stunner.

From time to time Butch encountered his girlfriend in the lobby, or occasionally on the elevator. These events triggered a great deal of hopping around, tail wagging, and much sniffing. Barking was frowned on and monitored. Their time together was usually limited. The daily walk was essential. Love affairs must wait.

Food was an important part of Butch's daily life. He ate any food offered to him. He believed in providing the very best cuisine for his dog. Butch's diet was carefully selected. Nutrition was not of high priority. Culinary selections included gourmet recipes from *CANIS MAGAZINE*. Butch was simply unable to avoid gulping down his meal the minute the bowl was placed on the floor in front of him. His owner occasionally became irritated about that. It was disrespectful of the fine cuisine he prepared for his pet dog. In addition, the dog never left any tips. This surely demonstrated a serious disrespect for elaborate services.

All this did not prevent his owner from spending a great deal of time on food selection and preparation. They were big productions. You may say the dog was overindulged. The old man could have written a bestseller dog cook book. It would have omitted suggestions about dieting. Butch grew fat. That did not bother his owner. A neighbor once commented the owner slavishly cooked all that dog food in order to also feed himself. He might have been right. The food looked so enticing, and every meal had to be properly tasted.

Butch entered dog heaven with a long sigh. Or perhaps he might simply have trotted up to the real heaven. It was probably the latter since the owner was so sure they would meet again. No one relishes the possibilities of entering dog heaven. His wife was in real heaven and would again be able to pat their loyal pet. This made the old man happy.

In the meantime, the owner continued his slow and solitary walks. He sorely missed Butch and no longer prepared those gourmet meals. He simply ate the fare in the community dining room.

ONCE UPON A TIME IN AN ELEVATOR

What better place for them to meet than on the north elevator of their retirement community. They had been residents of their community for some five years. During that time they had oddly failed to meet socially or formally. Yet their vision and tastes were quite focused. Day and night they bypassed one another.

Then it happened, on a day and time that will be long remembered. They both entered the same elevator at the same time. Things clicked, thoughts raced, smiles were genuine, and words were scant. They simply knew they shared a message that would immediately resonate.

What caused this elevator event? Perhaps it was the air inside the elevator, or the elevator speed, or a failure to properly scan the events bulletin board hanging on the wall. Elevator transportation in their community was swift. That did not matter. What did was that they had finally connected. Over the years he had learned that elevator rides required riders to communicate quickly and to come to the point. He got to the point.

They warmly greeted each other. This was followed by words that gave the impression they wanted to build a sincere friendship. From then on thoughts about future encounters would fill their hearts.

The next step in serious retirement community etiquette required him to invite her to dinner. It was assumed they would eat in the community dining room. This event very definitely suggested a non-pizza evening. The chef never served pizzas on Saturday evenings. They enjoyed a quiet dinner early one Saturday night. Other dinner residents periodically glanced at them and made comments throughout their meal.

They were in their late seventies. She came from Chicago, but never gave the impression she was a slick city type. No, she was polite, polished and gracious. He came from the Northwest and gave the impression he had found himself a delightful elderly companion. Northwesterners are noted for their good pickings when it comes to apples and women.

They both had distinctive white hair, which did not distinguish them from the other residents. They had uncommon good looks which is where their distinctiveness definitely showed up. They both looked young for their ages. But not so young that others would think they had not reached the mandated minimum admission age for their retirement community.

He was reminded that loving and caring couples frequently held hands. That activity was also a significant dissimilarity compared to the practices of others in the community. She had a beautiful smile which would brighten up any room. It helped that they both had active lifestyles. All this indicated their togetherness would remain. It did.

They soon began sharing the Community's activities, went bowling, ate ice cream, helped organize a dog beauty contest, and enjoyed occasional lectures. Hand in hand they rode the elevators. They never talked politics. Both attended church as often as possible. They shared their lives and proved that elderly folks can take pleasure in enduring romances.

Their love grew. They enjoyed the opportunities of retirement living, and dining with all their friends. They argued once in a while, yet they celebrated their close bonds every day. Each evening ended with a lengthy phone conversation. Their future would be a happy one.

"There goes old what's his name again!"

"All my life I was taught how to die as a Christian, but no one ever taught me how I ought to live in the years before I die."
—Billy Graham

CHAPTER FIVE

CRUISING INTO THE SUNSET ON BOARD A RETIREMENT COMMUNITY LINER

"CCRCs ARE CRUISE SHIPS THAT NEVER LEAVE PORT"

The above is an oft-stated cliché that seems to be a reasonably accurate analogy. The nautical relationship might be an appropriate association. It reminds some that residency in a CCRC is akin to cruising on a ship. To others it may be a poor comparison since not all such communities can be so characterized. Neither can all ships be compared to CCRCs. Ships do not have an assisted living facility, just a lot of lifejackets and sea air. Someone will remind you that both can sink when the navigation is sloppy.

If retirement community living resembles living on board ship, then when do CCRC residents receive assurances they can reasonably quickly and economically disembark from their landlocked ship? It is difficult to readily disembark from a CCRC for such reasons as the pool water is too salty, the seas are too rough, or the facility has sprung a leak.

Dissatisfied ship passengers quickly disembark at the end of a disappointing cruise. Their next cruise will probably be on another vessel. The financial consequence would be small, even after twenty cruises. If you cannot take a cruise for justified reasons you can collect on trip insurance. This sounds more like the residency terms of an assisted living community, and not a CCRC.

This leads to an examination of the CCRC way of contracting with retirees. Contracts may limit the percentage of down payment cash to be refunded to the resident. Variable terms may apply on the time allowed to reimburse a monetary entitlement following the departure of a resident from his apartment. Check what you agree to, why and how. In spite of all this the preponderance of landlocked residents are contented cruisers enjoying fair skies and calm seas.

This narrative encourages retirees to investigate assisted living facilities, and not focus exclusively on CCRCs. Reflect on the thought that only CCRCs provide skilled nursing facilities. This can become extremely important to a retiree in the long term.

The Federal Tax Code requires not-for-profit CCRCs to provide continued occupancy to residents who can no longer afford to pay their monthly fee. This is residential security. Cruise lines do not provide continuing occupancy on their ship, unless you keep reserving space until the ship gets scrapped, or you do. CCRC managements do place eligibility conditions on resident admissions. These and other contingencies should be investigated when researching retirement community living. Do not compare retirement communities to freighter cruises. They have upper-end age restrictions and infrequently provide medical care. But then who wants to cruise on a cargo ship?

Some residents draw the line when the bar on their stationary cruise ship runs out of champagne during a happy hour. Management may make amends by scheduling periodic wine-tasting gatherings. These well-attended soirees enable a retiree to become a wine connoisseur and tipsy, all at the same time. In past years, some residents may have been served "unlimited" free drinks at the happy hour. Cost containment forced some operations to limit free drinks to a single glass per evening. You pay for all your drinks on cruise ships. Either way, happiness is undiminished, and cruise residents eventually give up complaining. CCRC resident turnover does guarantee a shorter community recollection of the good old times.

In addition to a Friday evening attitude modification hour there are four other venues for CCRC gossiping sessions. The others are daily breakfast, afternoon tea, when traveling on an elevator, and particularly during lifeboat drills. If you strongly believe you live on a stationary cruise ship you need to know that the *most* intriguing location for gossiping is during lifeboat drills, particularly between lifeboats 6 and 8. They are both located amidships and on the starboard side. There are no couches to sit on, and they do not even have a standup bar.

Gossiping sites provide residents with an opportunity to assiduously debate five key topics.

- Dining-room food and service.
- Health issues, including care outcomes.
- Management and staff, and where they obviously erred.
- Who said what and to whom? Few really fathom why.
- Scary floundering ship tales.

Even fervent arguers fail to cobble common agreement with others. This facilitates friendships. Creating and spreading rumors can flourish during the happy hour (lifeboat drills). Topics have included sizing up an option that management will provide more than one free drink at the happy hour, or "Did you hear the ship is skipping the next port of call?" This gets the whole place keyed up. Most residents simply chuckle. Tattling is frowned on.

The question of the quality and variety of dining-room service and the cuisine are mainstays of resident chatter. This subject is fair game. Menus receive scrutiny. The topic of food provides a strong marker of resident satisfaction. It can be a strong satisfier or dissatisfier. Spaghetti is very tasty, and so are hot dog. Both are fattening.

REVISITING THE RETIREMENT BUSINESS

There is added value in re-examining several facets of the operational side of the retirement business. Two of the largest retirement operations in the industry have 870 communities, including approximately 86,000 residents. Both these firms have operated successfully for over 30 years. This is a big business and growing. There are many variations of retirement community facilities in this country, including elegant places, full service, or simply monthly fee. There are old and new ones, and facilities that occasionally become financially strapped. This has added to the history of caregiving. And now the baby boomers have come along and impact the industry in other ways.

What have we learned from past industry performance? Are results fulfilling sales presentations? Have essential services been delivered in key areas of resident care? What might managers learn from their previous work experiences and performance? What might industry, state governments, and advocates attempt to do to resolve perceived needs? What should state agencies not become involved in?

A number of salient factors influence the drive for successful retirement community management and operations. They include:

- The ability of an entity to better balance profitability with highest possible levels of healthcare, residential services, and benefits.
- The ability to balance a managing process that enforces strict community policies, and simultaneously creates a feeling among residents that they are "living in their old homes."
- The ability to foster continuing positive resident attitudes even after extended residency in a CCRC.
- A local labor market that provides a stream of qualified and competent employees to maintain continuing high levels of performance.
- The need to sustain profits (or minimize losses) during adverse economic times.
- Coping with inadequate financial resources to ride out facility startups or expansions.
- The ability to provide a continuing levels of care and services to residents so they feel they are receiving fair value for their investments. This includes a couple who spent $850,000 to move into their retirement apartment and now pay $6,950 a month to occupy their apartment. Might they have been better off by renting?

Retirement industry strategies are occasionally flawed. Retiree demographics are incorrectly estimated or interpreted. Some owners may too infrequently doubt their decisions.

REVISITING PERSONAL RELATIONSHIPS

This book described people events in retirement communities. It portrayed lifestyles, idiosyncrasies, and challenges. Some retiree behaviors were previously described in both glowing and chiding terms, with candor and tongue-in-cheek.

The writer does not wish to imply that the retirement community he lives in is in any way on the ropes or poorly managed. It is not. The typical mood remains tranquil and satisfying.

Retirement community living can occasionally be reflective and wistful. Homesickness and thoughts about the "Good Old Days" perk up alongside laughter and amusement. That is life. The following are some underlying causes of occasional resident irritability, frustration, or sadness.

Retirees are separated from their beautiful homes after deciding to experience the trauma of a final move. Dad no longer enjoys his spouse's exquisite gastronomy. Perhaps Mother buried Dad shortly before she moved into her apartment. She now pines for him and the happy family days of past years. The furniture does not properly fit into the new apartment's space. Relatives live far away and visit infrequently. A resident can no longer drive his car. Another is becoming more debilitated. These conditions and others may cause negative attitudes, or provoke irritable feelings. A resident may be further tempted to find fault with community life, management, or another resident.

Few appreciate the social side of a retirement community better than longer-time residents. Over time they have experienced reductions in resident services, and the costly comings and goings of staff. There is little worse that having excessive employee and resident turnover.

During the joy of living in a retirement community a resident may have run his life savings down to zero and declared bankruptcy. His children become unhappy executors. To save face, they tell their friends that he took it to heaven with him.

Interesting stories about the practices and features of competing retirement communities are periodically whispered around. A resident occasionally passes on competitor scuttlebutt to the marketing department. Others pass on sales leads. Competition is serious in this industry. Retirement community owners become envious of facilities that have a five year long new resident waiting list.

The available levels of healthcare service remain important in any retirement decision. Approaches to retirement community living will evolve in the ambitious push towards faultless care for the elderly. The industry will continue to secure a broader and stronger consumer following. It will further enhance an already positive public image.

WORDS OF A PAST SCEPTIC

Many retirement guidebooks utilize comparative tallies or narratives to assess this industry and its individual facilities. In contrast, this book has placed an emphasis on the societal aspects of retirement living. The book was not intended to be an exposé.

The author's focus was rarely *prescriptive* in its context, such as an attempt to tell retirees what they must do and when. It has largely avoided being *diagnostic,* through attempts to analyze what has failed, why, how much and how. A few narratives have gingerly infiltrated both these analytical techniques. The book's purpose is educational. It sought to provide broad insights for those interested in the CCRC.

Writing **Here Today and Perhaps Tomorrow** presented opportunities. A measure of evenhandedness was required as observations were made on a number of retirement situations. The cartoons were added for humor and absurdness. The use of vignettes, anecdotes, and narrative styles facilitated descriptions of life among good friends and caring staff. It also described life and circumstances beyond the portals of retirement communities.

Chronicling the CCRC scene is good for the memory, and needed mental exercise. Learning about what happens at other retirement communities increases one's perspectives, and appreciation. There are lighter and darker realities to the retirement business. Recognition of these facets is needed to gain a clearer picture of community living.

This book may enhance the consequences of a reader's later retirement. His life will be influenced by his chosen surroundings during the remaining years of his life. He may opt to move into an elegant community. Or to move into a retirement home close to O'Hare Field where he can listen to jet aircraft as they take off and land all day. Nothing is perfect, not even jet noise.

There is no perfect time to write a book on retirement communities, except now. It is certainly too late to begin writing after being moved into a memory support center. At that point you may probably not appreciate reading about retirement care for the elderly. Your memory is bad after you have forgotten how bad your memory used to be.

I earlier expressed skepticism about the prearranged and structured caregiving that some retirement communities offer to the elderly. With inherent doubts I continued to reflect on the quality of life in a skilled nursing facility. In spite of my stubbornness, it was impossible for me to remain indifferent to this ever-present mode of retirement care. So I knowingly made the transition from a satisfied life on a small island to contented life in a large CCRC. There was no turning back. My continuing friendly encounters have generated positive feelings. All this helped create the license needed to write about the retirement community phenomenon. Residents at my retirement community will now know why I lived a more secluded life for a year and a half!

Retirement community living will continue to thrive as the elderly age. At some time in the future some residents of a retirement community may exceed the age of 105 years. Professional and careful retirement community care can do wonders to prolong life. If you doubt this check geriatrics statistics.

An admonishment to grandchildren: Start saving your money. It is never too soon. By the time you begin researching retirement communities, the industry will have introduced new operating models. This may include further discounting. Prices and fees will definitely increase.

Feelings about his age might prompt a retirement community resident to think about how decrepit he is. An elderly resident, after reading the periodic announcements about the demise of his friends, will begin noticing that the year of his own birth progressively creeps closer to the years of birth of his dying friends. This is not a blunt reminder that he should have avoided living in a continuing care retirement community.

The most incapacitated souls make the best of it. We are often mildly exuberant, frequently delighted, and unusually optimistic about living and ageing. We occasionally suffer pain and frustration. This does not mean we will not be here tomorrow.

Retirement community residents expect to continue entertaining the outside world with their tongue-in-cheek stories.

They are proud members of a unique retirement lifestyle. We are aware that bystanders observing this retirement lifestyle will continue to witness the fact that elderly survivors inevitably fade away laughing.

"Never lose sight of the fact that old age needs so little but needs that little too much."
—Margaret Willour

LOVE IS FOREVER

He was born a Texan, yet he never lost his Texas accent. They were introduced to each other many years later in a small central Texas town.

She was born of Italian parents in Fernay, a small Italian village in the Val Grisance. Their daughter was an only child. Her family moved to America in 1936. She was seven years old and spoke no English. Three years earlier her Uncle Giovanni had also emigrated from Italy to Texas. He was now the chef in an authentic Italian restaurant in downtown Cleburne, Texas. Her family also settled in this small Texas town.

A family tradition was established. On most Sunday evenings they gathered at Giovanni's home to enjoy a pasta dinner. He expertly fixed the food. The family never believed Uncle Giovanni when he told them those hot and humid Texas summer days were the main reason he became so attracted to Texas. They occasionally told Giovanni his opinions about the weather would never convince other Italians to immigrate to Texas. The family initially felt strongly about living in Cleburne for the rest of their lives.

She made friends easily and learned to speak "Texas English." Friendly chattering had quickly taught her more than the basics. The locals seemed to speak strange sounding English, compared to some other people she listened to. She quickly learned "Howdy folks, how ya'all doin'?" Once in a while she tried to teach her friends a few Italian phrases. It did not work too well with a Texas accent.

His family moved to Texas from far-off Springfield, Massachusetts. The father found a farmhand job. Hard work, savings, perseverance and a loan from friends and the bank enabled them to purchase a small farm outside Texarkana, Texas. Arable land became the source of their livelihood. It was also the cause of reoccurring sore muscles.

There was a plentiful supply of wild turkeys in the vicinity of their farm. The son eventually taught himself to be a skilled turkey hunter. The family dog faithfully executed his required duty to flush out the game. He would have been unhappy if the local turkey population had ever run out.

His sisters helped their mother. They potted the best jams in town. Texas barbecue dinners began to replace pasta and tomato sauce. They helped their father outdoors.

On many evenings, his parents sat quietly on the porch and watched all those striking sunsets. They always held hands and were so grateful for their family.

His family clearly recalled the Great Depression. They remained frugal. To extend the family's income, one daughter helped her mother sew clothes for neighbors. From a young age he had learned to drive a tractor, manage a plough, and keep a trained eye on the direction of both tractor and plough. This combination created straight furrows to grow the crops that helped bring in money to feed the family during good and worse times.

Schooling came easily to him. He learned quickly and graduated at the top of his high school class. She also did well in school.

Her strengths included athletics. A letter of acceptance arrived admitting her to the University of Texas. She began participating in the school's sports program. She excelled in language studies. Meanwhile, he studied at the same university and thrived on mathematics and girls. Studying was challenging. His grades indicated he would be a good student. He became president of the Student Horticultural Society. Early on, the family realized he would eventually turn his back on farming.

He graduated. This was followed by the declaration of War. So the twenty one year old decided to enlist in the Marines. She continued her studies. Boot camp came and went. He was transferred back to Texas. His striking Marine figure made his family proud. The Marine once again turned out to be an accurate shot with a rifle. This time it would have more serious implications. His commanding officer wondered where he had developed his skill. He told him there were no more wild turkeys around the farm he had lived on. All of them were eventually shot. On the other hand, some had deserted the neighborhood for a safer life.

A significant event then occurred in his life. He met his future wife in the town he was stationed in before shipping out to the Pacific. She was on her way to Dallas to participate in a swim meet. They met in an Italian restaurant where several University of Texas friends had arranged a social gathering. She was shy. Both smiled warmly at each other. It was love over a bowl of linguini. Meetings continued as often as the Marines allowed, which was not often.

He wrote her many loving letters to her during his Pacific combat experience. They were mailed from a ship, from barracks, another ship, and after landing at Iwo Jima. The Marine vowed he would love her forever. He proposed to her in one of his more romantic compositions. She eagerly accepted. Their letters always reminded them how much they missed one another.

They married in Dallas, within a few weeks of his discharge from the Marines. The wedding was a small event. Chianti was served. The dancing went on and on. A friend read this short poem during the event.

"Like sweet milk and honey,
In union and fidelity,
Like bread and wine,
May your marriage be full of joy and much laughing?
Your every day is paradise,
You are GOD's gift to each other."

The honeymoon was in East Texas. He returned to university, graduated and then enrolled in a Ph.D. program. Mathematics again became a favorite subject. She found them a small apartment to live in, and began teaching at an elementary school

A beautiful baby arrived. There was nothing mathematical about the creation of that event. Two more babies arrived later, all of them were males. The three boys would have made a successful working party on the family farm.

The father earned his Ph.D. He was recruited for a teaching job at the University of Chicago. His wife often wondered why they had to move so far north. She preferred the Texas climate. A teaching position became available to her.

Their lives settled into a circle of quiet and conventional living, largely insulated from the outside world of campus demonstrations and counterculture. Their world was centered on love for each other, and love for their families. He always rooted for the Dallas Cowboys. She never disputed that.

Several years later he decided to relinquish his teaching career. A timely opportunity presented itself at a software design company in California. She encouraged him to make the change. They drove to the West Coast in his 1961 Chevy Impala, without a single flat tire.

The technical work challenged him, and he quickly learned the business. Promotions gradually followed. The years passed. She gave up teaching and focused on planting flowers and guiding three sons through their schooling. Family discussions helped them sort out changing priorities. They traveled, and purchased mementoes of their trips. Some were much too expensive for their check books. Both enjoyed their trips to Europe and Texas. Visits to Italy were for culture and her family reunions. Their travel to East Texas was for more family gatherings, barbecue and a brisk walk around the farm. He checked for wild turkeys.

He was eventually promoted to head the research department of his company Their sons moved out. They graduated from university, found jobs, and married. She occasionally wished one child would have been a girl.

The parents became grandparents. A routine of visits to expanding families had begun. Life settled down, accompanied by church, the golf course, the symphony, the flu season, and their dog. A parrot talked its way into the family picture. Political conversations were avoided. They often reminded themselves of their deep love, and spoke openly about their undying affection for each other.

Life was good to them. They had good health. An exciting event was to move into a larger house. This only made sense when children, grandchildren and close friends visited. He continued to brew coffee in the morning and his wife baked rhubarb pie every week. The father was now the head of a close-knit family. He enjoyed the respect of his community. They supported charities and became increasingly involved in their church and community affairs. Their marriage continued to blossom, and everyone said their union was created in heaven.

They moved beyond middle age. More grey hairs appeared. Her visits to the beauty salon increased, or so it seemed. He used his Exercycle more frequently. One morning he told her they were candidates for Social Security. She did not think much about it. He reminded the board of directors they should begin grooming his successor. They continued their volunteer work and went on periodic diets. Trips took them to warmer places. Their sons sometimes worried about their parents' health. One son told his friends his parents were securely connected at the hip.

He retired and began adjusting to a new lifestyle. They remained in their big house. He gave up mowing the lawn. A golf cart became his first means of mobility enhancement. Bridge became a greater part of their lives. He dabbled more in the stock market and honed his computer skills. She continued to enjoy social work and long phone calls with family and friends. They often chatted about their grandchildren. Reminiscing was more frequent. Life started to move into a lower gear.

He eventually told his wife he really was slowing down. She expected him to say he definitely felt older. He tired more easily. She told him not to worry and that she loved him just as much. They hugged and went their social ways. One morning they talked about selling their home. The discussion did not develop any further since they were leaving the next day for Paris. He became overtired as the trip progressed.

Old age had always seemed to be a far off thing to both of them. They admitted to themselves and their family that their bones were stiffening. She developed more chest colds. His high blood pressure had to be further medicated. She took more naps, and his prostate began to bother him. Doctor visits increased and a hospitalization or two modified their lifestyles. The family was increasingly concerned about their parents' health.

They wanted to remain in their large family home for a few more years. He was close to eighty. Time had slowed his walk. She fell and broke a hip. He increasingly searched for medical diagnoses and their explanations on the Internet. He took extra efforts to tend to his ailments. She began to check on the toxicity of their prescription drugs. An entire closet shelf was dedicated to old prescription containers.

He was advised his congestive heart failure was deteriorating. It bothered him. His wife worried. He knew drugs would not always treat his condition. She suggested they consider moving into a retirement community. His replied they would never move into one of those places. She chided him, replying that they had not visited any of them. This triggered many discussions, culminating in phone calls and several visits to attractive properties.

They made several emotional decisions, resulting in important changes. This included selling the home and relocating to a large retirement property. Their lives entered another phase. Both hoped their social needs would not require too great a readjustment. They made the move.

The pair settled into an 11th floor apartment in a northern California CCRC. Downsizing was challenging. They adjusted and made new friends. Travel was more limited. Church continued to be a regular event. Once in a while they tried to convince other family members to follow suit. Both spoke frequently and quietly to God.

Several years of quiet and secure apartment living followed. Their health had its ups and downs. They enjoyed the symphony, eating out, and family visits. Life in their retirement was pleasant. They continued to savor their loving companionship. She knew his heart condition would eventually require a higher level of care. They re-inspected the skilled nursing center and asked questions. She delayed transferring him there for as long as they could. His health eventually turned for the worst.

When his relocation day arrived they moved him into room 604. His wife tenderly accompanied him and carefully stored away a few favorite items. She visited him daily. They tried to make things look the same. She committed a great deal of her energies to caring for him. She fussed over him and brought him news of the outside world. Once in a while she took him for a short ride in their car. He became less agile at opening the car door and helping her get in. The family visited regularly. This helped compensate for his feelings of boredom. The grandchildren made him laugh.

Life continued at a slower pace. He was now in a wheel chair. He lingered on. She anticipated and relished hearing the tender words he so often whispered to her during their many years together. They were simply that he would love her forever. She smiled sweetly, with tears in her eyes.

OH! I ALMOST FORGOT!

While completing this book the author was prompted to reflect on his words about the quality, standards, and features of critical care in CCRC nursing centers throughout the United States. Care varies. It should be noted that references to CCRC competency and services are germane to Hospice organizations and their care for the dying.

The preceding vignette, its earlier counterpart, and other narratives have characterized several aspects of skilled nursing. They depicted poignant and edifying features about care in a nursing environment.

How might such narratives be made to resonate more clearly through some added thoughts about CCRCs?

Old age is an individual and personal circumstance of life. The elderly are trusting. They maintain their hopes. As they decline, they might even take great pleasure in their expectations. As they wane, they visualize compassion, consistency, and a growing dependability on others involved in their lives.

CCRCs have become an important aspect of elderly caregiving. The ultimate proficiency and critical values of a CCRC can be reflected in the competency of its skilled nursing center. It is indicated by staff performance at all employee levels. These requisites are even most relevant in the delivery of care for the long term, custodial patient.

New CCRC residents relocate into a community with high expectations, involving all services and features involved their future residency. They expect the CCRC will fulfill its corporate obligations and provide appropriate levels of caregiving. Management skills are constantly tested by the obligation to manage costs, while delivering optimal healthcare. The outcomes of such caregiving challenges are important indicators of long-term customer satisfaction.

These management challenges are reflected in the authentic values, performance standards, and results of the CCRC approach to elderly care. This matters to all retirees, as well as to community managements.

Offering fine food, excellent housekeeping, transportation and diverse activities are important services to residents. These services are immediately important to new arrivals at a CCRC.

The true test of a CCRC is linked to the standards and sustained quality of extended caregiving offered to debilitated patients in their facility. It is concurrently linked to the extended business survival of these operations.

A CCRC resident previously spoke about the care her spouse was receiving in a skilled nursing care facility. Her comments were realistic, insightful, and relevant to the realities of his care. In a practical way, she reminds us that it is unrealistic for new arrivals in a CCRC to visualize their eventual incapacity, or the full extent of the care they will receive.

Coping with dire infirmities is surely a question involving the patient and his Maker, and not simply linked to the quality of a patient's nursing care.

Here are the resident's own words.

"We coped while my husband eventually received long-term care in the Nursing Center. We witnessed, along with our newfound friends over there. As time passes, the inevitable developments of ageing must occur. We both regarded this as a natural process.

We cannot recall ever reading any retirement community literature that alluded to the extremes of final infirmities, and resulting care. That was impossible. So we used our own imaginations. That subject was far from uppermost in our minds."

CPSIA information can be obtained at www.ICGtesting.com
Printed in the USA
BVOW04s0028181213

339198BV00006B/207/P